Escape from Kabul

Escape from Kabul

*Eberhard Muehlan
with the Shelter Now team*

STRAND PUBLISHING

Sydney

Escape From Kabul
Copyright © 2003 by Shelter Now

First published as *Gefangen in Kabul* (Schulte & Gerth, 2002)
© 2002 Gerth Medien GmbH, Asslar

Revised English edition first published by Strand Publishing 2003
Translated from German by Cynthia Cave

ISBN: 1876825162

Distributed in Australia by:
Gary Allen Pty Ltd
9 Cooper St
Smithfield NSW 2164
Phone: 02 9725 2933
Fax: 02 9609 6155

Quotations from the Bible (some paraphrased) are from *The Holy Bible:
New International Version*. Copyright © 1973, 1978, 1984 by the
International Bible Society.

Cover photo courtesy of Associated Press

Edited by Owen Salter
Cover design by Joy Lankshear
Typeset by Midland Typesetters
Printed in Australia by McPherson's Printing Group

Contents

Acknowledgements

During our time in prison, we were aware that many people were working to secure our release, and many churches around the world were praying for us. But it was only after it was all over that we began to realise the full extent of the unceasing efforts that had been made on our behalf, far greater than we could ever have imagined. We are deeply indebted to all those who were involved.

It would be impossible to list all the names, but we would like to take this opportunity to pick out a few.

Our sincerest thanks go to the staff of the German, US and Australian diplomatic missions in Islamabad for all their efforts on our behalf. In particular we are grateful to those who came to Kabul in a very tense situation to negotiate with the Taliban—Mr Helmut Landes, the Embassy Counsellor from the German embassy, Mr David Donahue, the US consul general to Pakistan, and Mr Alastar Adams, the consul from the Australian High Commission. In addition to thanking Mr Landes and his wife, the four of us from Germany would also like to thank the German ambassador to Pakistan, Dr Christoph Bruemmer, and his wife.

Thank you, Mr and Mrs Bruemmer, for taking us into your home when we arrived in Islamabad and for lavishing your hospitality on us. Heartfelt thanks, too, to Ms Erna Salimi from the German embassy in Kabul—your commitment and visits in the Kabul prison greatly encouraged us.

We will forever be indebted to the men of the US Special Forces operation who rescued us. We are immensely grateful to you and full of admiration for your courage.

We would also like to thank the people of Ghazni who helped and supported us.

Our thanks to the German Foreign Office in Berlin, and in particular the crisis response centre there. Thank you, Mr Winkler and Mr Fahrenholtz, for making yourselves available to our German Director, Udo Stolte, at all times and for working tirelessly to secure our release.

The dedication of the Shelter Germany team in Braunschweig was phenomenal. For months on end they laboured day and night, mobilising the media and Christians throughout the world and constantly keeping them up to date. There was no let-up even after our release—they were left without a minute to themselves. Thank you, Udo, Siggi, Joe and the whole team there in Braunschweig.

We are also grateful to the Christuszentrum in Braunschweig and the pastor there, Horst Werner; to North City Christian Centre in Perth and Pastor John Finkelde; and to all the churches, Christian associations and individuals worldwide who prayed for us. We cannot personally thank the millions who prayed, but we are deeply grateful to them all for their concern.

A big thank you to Erik and Jeltje Spruyt and all the staff at Le Rucher who provided us with such an excellent counselling service and support immediately after our release.

There are so many personal friends we would also like to thank. Sadly, only a few of them can be named here: Chris and Antoine van den Assem, Greg and Shelvi Gilmore, Len and Diane Stitt, and all the Shelter team members in Pakistan and Afghanistan. We are utterly indebted to our Afghan staff, particularly those who were imprisoned, and to Hakim and Randall.

We are extremely grateful to the author of this book, Eberhard Muehlan, and his family. Our thanks also go to our English translator, Cynthia Cave.

We would like to thank our parents, brothers, sisters and other family members who worried about us and prayed for us desperately. To my own family, Marianne, Dani and Benni—thank you that you never stopped believing we would be reunited again.

Finally, we are profoundly grateful to God. It was he who preserved us, who gave us strength to keep going day after day, and who worked the many miracles that brought about our rescue. Our ultimate thanks go to him.

Georg Taubmann
and the Shelter Afghanistan team

Foreword

The Taliban's arrest in August 2001 of eight foreign aid workers—four Germans, two Australians and two Americans—was international news for more than three months. Only the terrible events of 11 September served to drown out their plight for a brief period. But as it slowly emerged that the Taliban had probably planned the arrests to use the aid workers as a bargaining tool to stave off US military aggression, the aid workers were once again back in the headlines.

When the military offensive in Afghanistan began on 7 October, all contact with the aid workers was lost. Western diplomats who had worked tirelessly for their release, friends and relatives who had worried and prayed for their safety—all knew they might never see them again.

Five weeks later, news of the aid workers' rescue by the US Special Forces came for their friends and co-workers in the West so suddenly and unexpectedly that at first we could hardly believe it. Unconfirmed reports of their release started to filter through on the evening of 14 November—it was a Wednesday and we were in fact in church praying for the situation.

By Thursday morning we knew for certain: all eight were free and unharmed. Those hours from the initial reports to the final confirmation seemed to drag on for an eternity and were extremely nerve-racking.

When I finally saw them, I greeted them all ecstatically, beginning with Margrit Stebner. Before going to Afghanistan, she had been my secretary for a number of years. I have known Georg Taubmann, the Director of Shelter Afghanistan, for over twenty years. We are close friends; my family and I had previously visited him in Pakistan, met the team there and visited the various refugee camps near Peshawar. Silke Duerrkopf is a member of my church and Katrin Jelinek is related to my daughter-in-law. When you have a personal friendship with the people involved in such traumatic experiences, you suffer with them in a way that is not possible when you just read about it in the newspaper.

Nevertheless, I was quite taken aback when they asked me to help them write a book about their story. 'Eberhard, you know us and our refugee camps, you're familiar with the culture in Asia,' they said, seeing my misgivings. 'We're not going to find it easy to talk about some of our experiences. We don't just want to tell any author about them. We trust you. You understand us.' And so I consented. As they began to talk, I was led into another world which both shocked and fascinated me: on the one hand, the brutality; on the other, the friendship of some of the Taliban guards. The deprivations of captivity, gruelling interrogations,

Afghan inmates who were outstanding personalities against all the odds. The agony, the desperate prayers, the hopes, the panic during the bombing raids, the breathtaking suspense during their abduction. And finally, the miracle of their liberation at Ghazni.

I have sought throughout the book to stay in the background and let the Shelter Now staff speak for themselves. It is important that you as the reader listen to them in person as they speak about their experiences, observations, feelings, fears, hopes and faith encounters.

In all the books I have published, I have never before found myself moved to tears while I wrote as I was on this occasion.

The eight aid workers would never call themselves heroes. But for me that is exactly what they are. They are also wonderful personalities who proved throughout the deprivations and dangers of their captivity that in the most difficult hours of our lives, God can be our security and comfort.

Eberhard Muehlan

The eight Shelter Now aid workers

GEORG TAUBMANN
Director of Shelter Now in Afghanistan. German, forty-five years of age. Eighteen years working in Pakistan and Afghanistan. Name pronounced 'Gay-org', but known to Afghans as 'Mr George'.

PETER BUNCH
Fifty-eight year old engineer from Australia. Working with project proposals and funding. Three-and-a-half years working with Shelter Now in Pakistan and Afghanistan.

DIANA THOMAS
Australian nurse working as Georg's secretary. Fifty years of age. Nine years working with Shelter Now in Pakistan and Afghanistan.

MARGRIT STEBNER
Georg's secretary for German correspondence. Forty-three years of age. One-and-a-half years working with Shelter Now.

SILKE DUERRKOPF
Thirty-six-year-old artist and teacher from Germany. Involved in home-schooling Georg Taubmann's children and in a Shelter Now street children's project. One-and-a-half years working with the organisation.

KATRIN (KATI) JELINEK
A German nurse of thirty-two years of age. Involved in the street children's project and an orphanage project. One-and-a-half years working with Shelter Now.

DAYNA CURRY
American, twenty-nine years of age. Joined the Shelter Now team three months before her arrest. Temporarily involved in the street children's project.

HEATHER MERCER
American, twenty-four years of age. Joined the Shelter Now team three months before her arrest. Studying local language.

Note: Six of the aid workers tell their story in this book. Dayna Curry and Heather Mercer tell their story in their own book, Prisoners of Hope. *Any differences between the two accounts are due to the fact that some names and details have been changed to protect individuals still living in Afghanistan.*

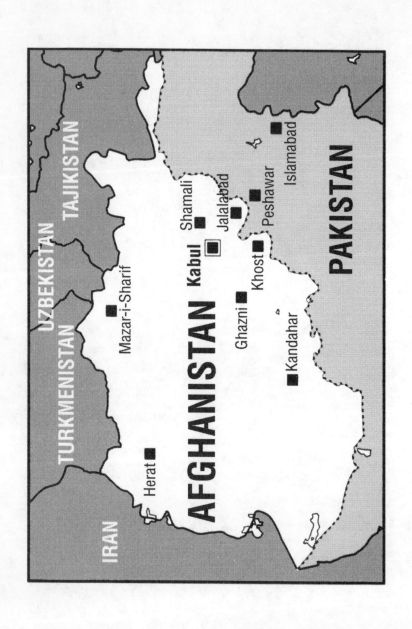

1

From Prisoners to Hostages

12 November 2001

The roar of fighter jets reverberated through the prison walls. Gunfire sounded much nearer and more frequent than in recent days. The walls shook, window panes rattled and the floor vibrated beneath the prisoners' feet.

Afghan inmates paced nervously up and down the corridor between the cells. The tension was almost unbearable.

For several days, Georg Taubmann and Peter Bunch—both aid workers from the organisation Shelter Now—had sat bent over a radio that had been smuggled into their Kabul prison. They were following the progress of Northern Alliance troops towards the capital. Things had moved more quickly than they had ever thought possible. Almost the entire north of the country as far as the city of Herat had been taken in just a few days. American jets had bombed the frontlines almost incessantly in the Shamali region to the north of Kabul. The aid workers hardly needed a radio to tell them that the city was about to fall to the Northern Alliance.

Their constant thought was how much longer it would take for the resistance fighters to reach the capital and free them. Or would the Taliban prison guards move them elsewhere first—or even kill them?

❧

GEORG TAUBMANN: 'Mr George!' asked one of the Afghan prisoners. 'Have you heard the latest? The Northern Alliance is just six miles from Kabul! Perhaps less!'

The Afghan prisoners discussed the various possibilities excitedly. About ten of them had received death sentences. Others were waiting for amputations—another form of punishment under the Taliban. These would have been the first ones to be killed by prison guards if it came to a surrender. Yet still they were concerned about our uncertain fate—that of myself, my colleague Peter who shared a cell with me, and our six women co-workers imprisoned on the floor above.

'If the Taliban try to do anything to you, we'll defend you,' declared Mustafa whose concern for us over the previous weeks had really touched me. He had become a genuine friend and was always hatching some new plan to get us out of that terrible prison. Once he had even arranged for someone to buy special saw blades at a local market and smuggle them into our wing of the jail.

'Here, I got these for you,' he said earnestly. 'We'll saw through the bars and get you out of here.'

'Mustafa, thank you that you're making such an effort on

our behalf,' I replied. 'But I really can't agree to this plan. I don't want anyone to be put at risk during the escape, and I certainly don't want anyone getting killed!'

Now he took me to one side, his voice pleading. 'Look, we're sure the Taliban will come for you and take you away. Who knows what they'll do with you then? They might kill you or take you to Kandahar.'

The mention of the Taliban's feared southern stronghold made my blood run cold. 'But what can we do?' I asked despairingly.

'Listen, we've come up with a plan. I've spoken to some of the guards upstairs and given them a bit of money. They won't stand in our way. They know it will all be over soon anyway. We've got three Kalashnikovs [Soviet-era machine guns] hidden in a cupboard. At eleven o'clock we'll go upstairs and spend the whole night up there. When the Taliban come, we'll overpower them and make off in their vehicles.'

Oh no, I thought, *there's no way this can succeed.* But I realised that nothing I could say would convince my friend to abandon his plan, so for the time being I remained silent.

By eight o'clock in the evening I felt severely agitated. No matter how hard I tried, I just couldn't see a way out of our situation. It was growing more dangerous by the hour. What should I do? The confusion and tension were such a strain on my nerves that I could hardly think straight any more. And yet I was the one who had to make the decisions. I was gripped by fear. After three-and-a-half months in prison, we were so close to being liberated;

what if something happened to one of us now? I didn't want to think about it.

The ceiling above me shook under the gunfire outside, even though our cell was a good two metres below ground. Beads of perspiration gathered on my forehead and I felt myself beginning to panic. In an attempt to calm down, I crawled into a niche in the wall.

'O God,' I groaned, 'don't let them kill us or take us away. Please don't let it be Kandahar!'

I was suddenly aware of a loud commotion outside in the prison courtyard. I heard orders being shouted, cars arriving and leaving again. I decided that valuable items and important documents were probably being taken away before the Northern Alliance arrived.

Something's going on, I thought. *I have to speak to the women. But how?*

I approached the prison guards and told them I had to go to the women to collect some medication. 'Diana is a nurse,' I explained.

One of them led me upstairs. I knocked on their cell door and quickly gave them my instructions, deciding to use German so the guard wouldn't understand me.

'The Northern Alliance is now only a few miles from Kabul. Something is sure to happen in the next few hours and then things could start moving very quickly.' I tried to speak as normally as I could for fear of disclosing my agitation to the guard. 'Barricade the door. Whatever happens, don't open it until you hear my voice. We need to do all we can to make sure we don't get separated.'

I then took the pack of medication and strolled back

downstairs with as much of an air of nonchalance as I could muster.

I was grateful the women had prevailed on the prison authorities to give them locks for the inside of their doors. I had just been able to warn them in time. At about 10.00 p.m. several cars pulled up outside. I heard footsteps passing through the entrance and then keys turning in the locks of the main gate. A noisy group of Taliban ran through the corridors and hammered on the door of the women's cell.

'Open up, open up! Come out here now!'

'No,' Diana replied firmly. 'We won't come out until you get Georg.'

Furious at not having their orders obeyed, the men hammered on the door all the louder.

'Fetch Georg and Peter and then we'll open the door.'

Diana knew all too well that the Taliban would have no difficulty in forcing their way in should they so decide. But she stood her ground. Surprisingly, the men finally acceded to her demand and stormed downstairs to fetch Peter and myself.

We had heard the men shouting and banging above us and were almost beside ourselves with worry. Suddenly we found ourselves staring down the barrels of several Kalashnikovs. We took one look at the tense faces of the Taliban and scrambled to gather our few possessions before following them back upstairs.

'Diana, Diana, open up quickly!' I shouted anxiously when we arrived at the women's room. 'They're serious. They're ready to shoot us!'

The women quickly opened the door.

'Get out here!' roared one of the guards. 'You don't need to bring anything with you. We're only taking you to a safe place for the night'.

But the women were not to be taken in. They had been lied to so often they were no longer prepared to believe anything. They quickly packed up their blankets and few items of clothing.

All eight of us were then hustled outside to two waiting vehicles. It became clear that the Taliban wanted to split us into two groups. We knew that whatever happened we had to stick together. In the three months of our imprisonment, one of my constant worries had been that something could happen to the women if they were to fall into the hands of vindictive Taliban while we men weren't around.

'We won't be separated,' I said firmly.

As time was now extremely short, the guards gave in to our demand. Clutching our few belongings, we clambered into the back of a Toyota Land Cruiser and flopped down onto the two rows of seats. One armed guard squeezed in with us, and it was only then that I noticed a number of mortars lying on the floor. Finally we moved off, sitting more on top of each other than side by side. The second vehicle, full of yet more armed Taliban, drove behind us.

Margrit Stebner: It was quite a shock when they came to get us out of our cell. These aggressive men appeared so suddenly from nowhere, with Kalashnikovs pointing right at us and ready to shoot. It was obvious they wouldn't have thought twice about it.

You never forget a look like that. Several hours before-hand I'd had a premonition that something bad was about to happen. Inwardly, I felt quite distraught.

I was the first one to get into the Land Cruiser and landed in a corner right at the front on top of the Taliban's luggage. Our belongings came next, by which point I was half buried. I could hardly move and found it difficult to get enough air. I was gripped by a sudden panic. I quickly realised that we were heading for Kandahar, although Georg evaded the question when I put it to him.

The whole thing seem so unreal and so frightening. All I could do was pray. And yet words seemed to fail me. I tried desperately to fight back my fears. And then, in the midst of all the confusion, I suddenly had an unforgettable experience. It was as if someone inside me was laughing. I felt an inner voice saying, 'You're on your way to freedom!'

That can't be true, I thought. But God suddenly felt very real and close to me. The sense of oppression and panic was gone.

∽

GEORG: *Where can they be taking us?* I wondered. *Another prison? Or somewhere else?*

First we drove into the city. I knew the area well. The driver tore down the streets, once nearly crashing into another vehicle. We drove past the Hotel Intercontinental, then down a street which led to a big silo.

And now I realised where we were headed. Next we would take the road to Wardak, from there to Ghazni and from there . . . to Kandahar.

The others were becoming agitated but managed to stay remarkably calm.

'Georg, do you know where we are? Tell us where we're going,' someone said.

I couldn't bring myself to say the chilling name. 'I think this goes to Wardak,' I said.

'And where is Wardak? Is that towards the Pakistani border?'

'No, not exactly.'

Kandahar. The mere thought of the southern Afghan city struck terror into my heart. When the Taliban conquered Kabul in 1996, Mullah Mohammed Omar chose this city on the edge of the Registan Desert as the power base from which he would rule Afghanistan. The Kandahar prisons were notorious. Anyone taken there abandoned virtually all hope of returning alive.

As we drove out of Kabul, I sat in the back of the Land Cruiser, totally exhausted and wretched. We had been whisked away just hours before the liberation of Kabul. We had dreamed of joining the other liberated prisoners and dancing in the streets to celebrate the end of Taliban rule. Now we were hostages—and headed for the worst place in all Afghanistan.

2

In the Snare of the Religious Police

The Shelter Now team in Kabul will probably never forget the first weekend of August 2001. In the eighteen years since the founding of Shelter Now in Peshawar, northern Pakistan, the organisation had gone through some hard times and its workers had faced life-threatening situations before. But nothing was on a par with this.

Their arrest, and the charges later brought against them, were linked to a visit made to an Afghan family. This particular family had repeatedly urged Kati Jelinek, Heather Mercer and Dayna Curry to visit them and show them a documentary film about the life of Jesus.

Kati had known the children—three girls and a boy, aged roughly four to twelve—for quite some time. She and Silke Duerrkopf had often visited their home in the days before they started giving out food to street children in Kabul. When their mother fell ill one day, the children came and asked them to visit her. They immediately consented, and Kati, who was a nurse, took her some medication.

It is impossible to visit an Afghan home without

staying to drink tea and talk with the family. Many Afghans are curious to know how people from the West live and whether they believe in a god. In the West, faith is often seen as a personal matter, and talking about it to others who don't share that faith tends to be frowned upon. But in Muslim cultures, talking about God and religion is the most natural thing in the world. Many are keen to know what the *khaarijees*—foreigners—believe, and very often they will try to convince the 'infidels' of their own Muslim faith. Most Afghans are quite taken aback when they discover their guest is also a believer —if not in Allah, then at least in the God of the Bible.

This was the case with Kati when, in response to the mother's questions, she said she believed in Jesus. Immediately, all the women in the family wanted to know more about this highly respected prophet in Islam. And as they were unable to read, they asked about the possibility of a film.

Shelter Now Under Fire

In 1990, Islamic extremists attacked and destroyed the Shelter Now aid project for Afghan widows and orphans in a refugee camp north of Peshawar, Pakistan. The care provided by aid agencies in general for women was evidently a thorn in the flesh to some Islamic extremists, and Shelter Now was not the only organisation to suffer. Other projects aimed at women and children encountered similar problems, including a school for girls.

A large factory compound where Shelter produced

roofing materials for refugee houses, along with a car repair shop, were destroyed at the same time. Everything, from their fleet of trucks to the most inexpensive items, disappeared. The destruction and theft cost the organisation more than US$1.5 million.

The Pakistani government conducted a thorough investigation of the plundering of Shelter Now property. The report concluded that the organisation had done nothing to justify such wilful destruction. The chief minister of the Northwest Frontier Province presented Shelter Now with a large sum of money and officially requested that it resume its work among Afghan refugees in Pakistan.

But there followed immediately an attempted assassination of the Shelter Now director. He and his young son escaped only by a miracle, and he was in shock and needed to leave the country with his family. More death threats followed. The decision was taken to freeze all project work and most of the Western staff left the country. It looked like Shelter Now as an organisation was finished.

But Georg Taubmann, at that time in Germany on home leave, was not ready to admit defeat. He often lay awake at night worrying about the plight of the Afghan women and children in the Pakistani desert without shelter or a regular food supply. He refused to give up despite the appalling injustice suffered by the organisation at the hands of religious fundamentalists. Ignoring the advice of concerned friends, he returned to Pakistan, was given the position of Shelter Now director, and began to rebuild the work from scratch.

Shelter Now again began distributing daily food rations to refugee families. Houses, clinics and schools were rebuilt in the refugee camps.

In 1992, Shelter Now decided to expand its work into neighbouring Afghanistan, beginning with a factory to make roofing materials for housing and outdoor bathroom facilities. In the following years, this initial factory was joined by four more.

The Shelter Now staff knew they were putting their lives on the line. Several times they got caught up in feuding between various tribes. On one occasion, when the team was returning to Pakistan after visiting a newly-built factory in the eastern city of Khost, they were kidnapped by a group of bandits a short distance from the border. Their captors were hoping for a hefty ransom. Fortunately, a group of passing Afghans recognised the delicate nature of the situation and managed—in typical Afghan style— to distract the kidnappers while the Shelter Now team made a successful bid for freedom.

On that particular Friday afternoon, 3 August, Kati needed time to prepare for a team meeting in the evening. So she asked Heather and Dayna to visit the Afghan family without her. The two Americans therefore went alone. They showed the women and children the film on their laptop, and Dayna gave the little boy—who was keen to learn English—a copy of a children's book in Dari and English.

Dayna then left early to go to another appointment.

❧

DAYNA CURRY: As I was due to meet someone else at half past four, I left the family on my own and took a taxi with one of our regular drivers. The car had just pulled up briefly at a junction when a man ripped open the front passenger door and shouted menacingly at the driver, 'Let me in!'

I was shocked when the taxi driver then just let the stranger get in—I was a woman travelling alone, sitting in the back seat.

'What's going on? Who are you?' asked the driver.

'Shut up!' the stranger bawled and turned to glare at me. His eyes were so full of hate I was initially silenced.

He pulled a walkie-talkie from his pocket and spoke into it. Seconds later a carload of Taliban drew alongside and a man with a gun climbed into the taxi next to me. With a growing sense of alarm I turned back to my driver.

'Please can you drive me to my organisation? I'm a woman alone. I'm afraid!'

He shrugged his shoulders nervously and ducked his head without replying. Suddenly a whole horde of Taliban surrounded the car.

'Where are the other women? Where is the equipment?' they demanded.

'I won't talk to you under these conditions,' I said, trying not to panic. 'Take me to my boss.'

They ignored me and made the driver keep going. We arrived at a government building in the centre of town and stopped. They bundled me into another car and the taxi sped away.

For two hours I sat there. My mind was racing. In

Afghanistan, women were often beaten in the street and taken away for no reason. What were they going to do with me? There was nothing I could do but pray. The waiting seemed to last forever.

Finally the taxi returned and I saw Heather sitting in the back seat, with another car full of Taliban in tow. I breathed a sigh of relief. Part of me wished she had got away, but I was grateful to no longer be alone.

&

Heather had sat with the family until they had finished watching the video. Then at about six o'clock she packed everything together and prepared to leave. The family were not as effusive in their goodbyes as usual, and they did not accompany her to the gate as they normally did. The crowd of noisy, happy children also stayed behind in the house. She was extremely surprised by this unexplained break with tradition.

Then she noticed a stranger sitting in the passenger seat of the taxi. *The driver's probably just bored and decided to bring his friend with him,* she told herself, trying to shrug off her suspicions.

'Did you have to wait long?' she asked the driver.

She got no reply. In the rearview mirror, she noticed the fearful expression on his face.

She had barely sat down in the back when the opposite door flew open and another man pushed his way into the vehicle. Alarmed, she tried to jump out. But the second man grabbed hold of her arm. More men appeared. This time they were clearly Taliban and carried Kalashnikovs. They surrounded the car. Heather had no choice but to sit tight and wait to see where they would take her.

After a short journey, she reached the other vehicle where Dayna was being held. Escorted by at least thirty armed Taliban, they were then driven to a women's prison.

∻

At around six o'clock, the Shelter Now team drifted in for their usual Friday night meeting. They spent the first hour chatting, drinking tea and enjoying a bite to eat. By seven the official part of the evening began with notices, practical instructions regarding work and a time of prayer and worship.

Several people began asking, 'Hey, Georg, do you know where Heather and Dayna are? They haven't arrived yet.'

'They're probably still visiting that family they told us about,' he said. 'I expect they're just a bit late.'

But privately, Georg agreed it was strange. *Oh well, these visits always take longer than planned*, he told himself. *First more relatives arrive, then the food isn't ready on time, and before you know where you are, the whole thing has taken two hours longer than you expected.*

But throughout the meeting, Georg found it hard to concentrate. He could not shake off the feeling that something was wrong. Margrit felt the same.

'Georg, we ought to do something,' she said.

Kati offered to drive to the Aghan family's house

with two of the men, Peter and Kurt, to see what was happening.

'Yes, please,' said Georg. 'It's getting to the point where we need to know.'

To avoid attracting attention, the three decided to leave their own vehicle behind and take a taxi. Arriving at the house of the Afghan family, they found a scene of considerable confusion. The neighbours stood around locked in anxious discussion.

'Well, at least there are no Taliban here,' said Kati, more to reassure herself than inform the others. The Taliban were always easy to spot by their standard uniform of turban and Kalashnikov.

After a while, several women came up to them all talking at once. Kurt, who had quite a good command of Dari, was only able to make out the words, 'Betrayal! Betrayal! They even took the men away.'

PETER BUNCH: When we got there, quite a lot of people were coming out of the houses nearby. When we eventually got to see the family, they were pretty distraught. They told us that two or three of their menfolk had been taken away, and that Dayna and Heather had been taken by the police.

It wasn't apparent at that stage, but later we realised that Dayna and Heather had been set up. But I think the Afghan family were forced into the deal. They were upset from both angles—from being set up themselves and from seeing the girls and their own men taken away by the police.

∞

The three quickly realised that the situation was serious. Maybe Heather and Dayna were being interrogated. Or even under arrest. They jumped back into the taxi and returned to the team.

Bursting in on the group, they broke the bad news. For a moment everyone was speechless. Georg broke off the meeting and asked them all to pray in small groups for Heather and Dayna.

After a while, he asked Kurt and Jonathan to drive him back to the Afghan family. 'Perhaps the women know more,' he said. 'Maybe they can tell me who came for Heather and Dayna, and where they're likely to be now.'

But the women were unable—or perhaps unwilling—to provide any more details. So the men drove to the police station responsible for that district. The officers on duty just stared at the foreigners in amazement. They knew nothing about any arrests.

It was already 9.00 p.m. and curfew started at 11.00. Georg racked his brains: *Who can help us now?* Suddenly he remembered. Haji Rashid! If anyone could help, it was him. Georg felt an immediate sense of relief. Haji Rashid was a high-level member of the Taliban with whom Georg had developed a real friendship over the past year. He would surely be able to use his influence to help the two women.

With the curfew fast approaching, the three men sped along the streets. But in the darkness they were unable to find the right house. Finally, they decided to drive to Haji Rashid's office instead. That proved easier to locate. Georg asked one of the guards there to jump in the car and show them the way to Haji Rashid's home. By the time they finally arrived, it was 10.00 p.m.

∽

GEORG: Forcing myself to regain my composure, I strolled into my friend's house—when you're with Afghans, you can't be in a rush. Haji Rashid was extremely pleased to see me.

'How are you and how is your family?' he asked, stretching out his arms in a welcoming gesture. 'Are you in good health?'

The typical Afghan greeting ceremony and exchange of pleasantries began. We sat down to drink tea. As I had just returned from a long stay in Germany, I first brought him up to date on our family news.

'And I've brought you a blood pressure gauge as a present from Germany, just as you requested,' I told him cheerfully.

During my time away, he had been involved in a car accident and now proceeded to fill me in on the details. I emphasised at great length how relieved I was that nothing terrible had happened. *Whatever you do, don't rush things,* I told myself. *Keep cool.* A surreptitious glance at my watch told me it was now half past ten.

Finally, I felt it was okay to risk telling him the reason for my late visit. 'Haji Rashid, something terrible has happened in our aid organisation and I am very concerned.'

'My friend, please tell me what has happened. Can I help you in any way?'

'Yes. Two of my staff visited an Afghan family this afternoon and were evidently arrested at some stage. I don't know why and I don't even seem to be able to find out where they are being held.'

'Mr George, that is terrible. I understand your concern. I'll try to find out what I can immediately.'

He strode over to the telephone, dialled a number and spoke with the air of one accustomed to having his authority respected. Throughout the call, I watched his face. As the conversation proceeded, his expression became more thoughtful, changing to concern and finally dismay.

Haji Rashid replaced the receiver and returned to where I was sitting with a look of consternation.

'Mr George, your two staff members have indeed been arrested.'

'But why?' I asked despairingly.

'They said it was because they showed the Afghans some kind of films. The worst thing is, it was the Vice and Virtue Police who arrested them. There I have no influence. All I could do was urge them to treat the women correctly.'

The Ministry for the Promotion of Virtue and Prevention of Vice—often dubbed the Vice and Virtue Police— was an independent body within the Taliban regime. It was subject directly to Mullah Mohammed Omar, the 'supreme leader of the faithful', and was feared by moderate Taliban and all other Afghans.

'Haji Rashid, thank you so much for doing me this favour,' I said. 'I am really very concerned. Thank you for using your influence to help us.'

'But of course, my friend. For you I am happy to do it.'

'May I come back to you tomorrow? Perhaps you will be able to find out more information by then.'

We arranged to meet again the next day and parted with another profusion of courtesies.

The Origins of the Taliban

Afghanistan's Taliban movement had its beginnings in Pakistan. Anyone who has received instruction in Sunni orthodoxy at one of the *madrassas* (conservative Koranic schools) is addressed as *Talib* (student), which in the plural form becomes *Taliban*.

Students at a *madrassa* would normally undergo an eight-year basic training course during which they would learn everything necessary to become a *Mullah* (Islamic cleric and scholar). Many Pashtun refugee families from Afghanistan sent their sons to these schools simply because they knew they would be fed and clothed there for free. In addition to religious instruction—which focused more on the Islamic law or *sharia* than on the Koran—the boys also underwent military training. Learning to read and write was not considered important. As a result, many of the Taliban are still illiterate today.

In the mid-1990s, Mullah Mohammed Omar, together with a large Taliban following, intervened in the power struggle between Afghanistan's various groups of Mujahedin (Islamic guerrilla fighters). In 1996, the Taliban captured the capital, Kabul. The Taliban quickly advanced across Afghanistan until they controlled at least 80 per cent of the country. Mullah Omar set up a pseudo-religious dictatorship based on an extreme interpretation of *sharia*, the Islamic law handed down since the early Middle Ages. He claimed to have created the purest Islamic state in the world.

After the Taliban came to power, they closed nearly all public schools as well as the university in Kabul. Films and television were prohibited along with photographs and all forms of music. Nearly every sport was banned, including soccer, kite-flying and keeping pigeons. All toys depicting humans or animals were forbidden.

Women and girls were stripped of nearly every basic human right, including the rights to work and to receive education. They could not leave the house unless fully veiled in the *burka*, a head-to-toe garment with only a mesh screen for vision. Even when wearing the approved clothing, women had to be escorted at all times in public by their husband or another male relative (even if he was only five years old). Though not officially allowed, it was often tolerated if women went out in groups. After more than twenty years of war in Afghanistan, very many women were left without husbands or any other male relatives. Life for these women in particular became all but impossible.

The Vice and Virtue Police patrolled the streets of Kabul daily. Women deemed insufficiently veiled were whipped on the spot. Men received similar treatment if their hair or beards were not the correct length. Shops were forcibly closed if their owners did not pay regular visits to the mosque. Men were beaten if they were caught not praying at the appointed times. Similar punishments were meted out both to men and women for all kinds of minor offences. Anyone caught stealing could have a hand or a foot amputated, sometimes both. Adulterers and apostates were executed.

Back out on the street, the three men climbed into the car. It was now just before 11.00 p.m., and violation of Kabul's curfew was a serious matter. Anyone caught on the street was immediately arrested. Georg was also uncertain whether all guards had been informed of a recent extension of the curfew from 10.00 to 11.00 p.m. Distracted by his concern for the women and yet driven by the lack of time, Georg raced through the streets, eyes peeled for checkpoints, until he finally turned into the entrance of his house. It was just after eleven o'clock.

∾

The night was to be a short one for Georg. There was no time to think about sleep. He turned the same questions over and over in his mind. How were the two women? Would other staff be interrogated? Would there be more arrests? Should he evacuate all the Shelter Now staff?

O Lord, he thought, *what if our whole project goes down the tube like in Pakistan eleven years ago?*

The following morning saw one crisis meeting after

another. Georg warned his staff to prepare for possible evacuation and pack an emergency suitcase so they could leave at a moment's notice.

'Please destroy everything that could possibly be viewed as offensive if your homes or offices are searched by the religious police. Remember, that could include even an advertisement in a Western magazine!'

Mullah Omar was continually announcing new decrees on Radio Sharia and it was impossible to remember everything. Only a short while before, a new law had been announced prohibiting foreign women from driving a vehicle (Afghan women were banned from driving already). Foreign women were not actually obliged to wear a *burka*, although there was always a concern that they might not immediately be recognised as Westerners if they went out veiled but without a *burka*. But even when they were recognised, they were often insulted and spat on by angry Taliban for wearing only a *chador* (a head covering consisting of a large shawl). The individual staff possessed Christian magazines, Bibles and music CDs in their own language for private use. Under normal circumstances these were permitted. But now they were cause for concern. Even *Time* magazine or other news journals could be viewed as subversive literature, depending on the mood of the Vice and Virtue Police.

After these staff meetings, Georg drove back to the office of his Taliban friend. Haji Rashid was not there, but he had left his deputy in charge. He too viewed the situation as very bleak, firstly because a religious CD had been found in the possession of the Afghan family and secondly because the Vice and Virtue Police had been behind the arrests. He was clearly torn between his desire to help Georg as a friend and his fear of incurring the wrath of the Vice and Virtue Police himself. Obviously he was unable to help them any further. So Georg asked him simply to pass on a bag of personal belongings to Heather and Dayna and said goodbye.

The mood among the Kabul team remained extremely subdued throughout that day and evening. The need to sort out various practicalities came as a welcome distraction from the dark cloud of uncertainty which now engulfed every team member.

PETER: I was shocked and angry at the arrests, but I realised these sorts of things were always possible with the way the religious police operated. I didn't expect Dayna and Heather to be imprisoned, though—just that they would get a rap over the knuckles or, in the worse scenario, be told to leave the country. Our main concern was to find out where they were being held.

Initially I had no real inkling that anyone else would be arrested. I thought our houses would probably be searched. Most of the Saturday was spent clearing computers and homes of any material the police might find suspicious.

KATI JELINEK: That Saturday evening I called my pastor in Germany. 'Thomas, perhaps what I'm about to say won't make any sense,' I told him, 'but two of our staff have apparently just been arrested. The Taliban may come looking for me too, because I had originally intended to join them in visiting an Afghan family. But if anything does happen, you don't need to worry. I'm prepared!'

I really was prepared too. Anyone who went to Afghanistan couldn't rule out these kinds of problems. That night, I went through all the risks in my mind and asked myself very honestly whether I would be ready to go through serious difficulties for the sake of helping the Afghans: interrogation, deportation or even imprisonment. At every point I was able to say yes.

This session of serious stocktaking was a real help to me later on and carried me through all the difficulties of imprisonment.

∽

At six o'clock on Sunday morning, Georg and his wife Marianne were startled by a sudden and incessant ringing of their doorbell. Marianne ran to the door and peered cautiously through the peephole.

'Can we speak to Mr George, please? It's urgent!' asked one of a group of Afghans standing outside.

'Georg, come quickly. There's a jeep full of men outside.'

Full of foreboding, Georg rushed out and opened the gate. But he immediately recognised the visitors as friends. They were clearly agitated and in a great hurry.

'Mr George, we have information that your office is

going to be searched today and things may get worse for you.'

Georg sensed that this was reliable information and thanked them profusely. They jumped back in the jeep and sped off in a cloud of dust.

In spite of all the bad things that we have to go through, there are still good people among the Taliban, he thought gratefully as he returned to the house.

By 8.00 a.m., all the staff had gathered for a meeting at the house shared by Georg's two secretaries, Diana Thomas and Margrit Stebner.

'I have reliable information that our main office will be searched today,' Georg told them, gravely. 'They may well decide to look through other buildings too. Be prepared to evacuate.'

At this point, no one was thinking that further arrests could be made.

'Please take care of any urgent matters you still have to attend to and be back here for our next team meeting at 2.00 p.m.'

That meeting was never to take place. During the next few hours, the team were overtaken by events.

First, Diana and Margrit were arrested in front of their office as they were about to collect money and important documents from the safe. Diana was able to warn the others on Margrit's walkie-talkie.

Peter, who was out with the Shelter Now's Afghan project manager, Gul Khan, heard the warning and drove straight to the office to see what was going on. Both were arrested on the spot. They had the privilege of driving themselves to prison as the Taliban had no vehicle with them.

Kati had gone to check on Shelter Now's street children's project just before the afternoon meeting. She had wanted to give the Afghan staff a few instructions and leave some money behind in case she had to leave Kabul suddenly. But the Taliban were waiting for her. She was then forced to take them to her home, where her ailing housemate Silke was virtually dragged from her sick bed by armed Taliban.

Finally, Georg, who had visited the Afghan Foreign Ministry, was on his way back when he decided to look in on Kati and Silke to check that everything was okay. He quickly regretted his decision. A group of Taliban were still guarding the house. They immediately dragged him into their car and took him off for interrogation.

The Children's Project in Kabul

There are an estimated 28,000 children earning their living on the streets of Kabul, some of them as young as two years old. Most are orphaned or fatherless. Some have fathers unable to work because of war wounds. They get nothing to eat at home apart from the odd piece of bread, so they spend their lives begging for food or money. They cannot go to school because their families rely on the money they earn from begging.

During their short existence, most have experienced

more death and destruction than the average Westerner in a lifetime.

At the time of the arrests, the children's project, led by Kati, had only been running for three months. After gaining permission from the appropriate ministry, a plot of land had been rented in May 2001. It had two large houses and enough space to run activities for 150 to 200 boys.

After intensive preparations—including input from leaders of other children's projects—workshops were set up where boys of all ages and abilities could make paper flowers and print writing paper using traditional Afghan wooden stamps. Silke had spent a long time collecting old stamps, repairing them and re-carving the shapes where the original ones had worn away. She had shown Afghan craftsmen her ideas so they could then work with the boys. The products were sold in the markets in Kabul. Some even went for sale in Pakistan.

The boys were able to come for one hour a day to work and earn money. Their only other means of supporting their families was the odd casual job, when they were lucky enough to get one. The rest of the time they resorted to stealing and begging. Much to her disappointment, Kati was unable to get permission to include girls in the project.

By the time she was arrested, Kati already had seventy boys on her books—all with the permission of their parents. She had also given employment to eight Afghan men. A few days before her arrest, a carpentry shop was

also opened, designed to provide work and eventually
training for older boys.

The project included a food and clothing program,
which had been started the previous winter. One morning,
Kati and Silke had found several boys sitting in front of
their house, lips blue with the cold and shivering all over.
They were dressed in thin T-shirts. The lucky ones had
plastic sandals; others were barefoot. Kati and Silke
immediately scraped together their own money to buy
second-hand shoes and clothing at the market. They took
the children into their home and gave them something
to eat.

Word of this soon got round. More and more children
began lining up outside the house each morning. Kati and
Silke were told by a Taliban official that they must not let
the children into their home, so they began feeding them
on the street. By the spring, up to sixty children a day
were coming to get bread, fruit and tea.

When girls came, Kati and Silke would sneak them
something secretly.

MARGRIT: It felt as if there was really something in the air.
The sudden arrest of two colleagues had come as a real
shock. Suddenly I found myself thinking, *What happens if
they decide to arrest me too?*

Before the meeting, Diana and I decided to take a taxi to
the office and quickly fetch some of our personal papers and
money from the safe. But when we arrived, we found the
gate locked and a group of Taliban standing nearby.

Not realising what was going on, we asked to be let into our office to fetch a few things.

'Wait here. Someone's just fetching the key for the entrance,' the apparent ringleader replied.

So we sent the taxi away and waited. In Afghanistan, patience is more than a virtue—it's fundamental to the retention of one's sanity.

But after about half an hour, we decided enough was enough. As the taxi was already gone, we started to walk back up the little street. We didn't get very far. Immediately, a group of men marched up behind us. We tried to ignore them, but when one of them barred our path with a whip swinging from his hand, we knew there was no way of escape.

'You can't leave,' he told us, moving his whip menacingly in our direction. 'Stay by the gate. You're going to be interrogated. We are only waiting for a vehicle.'

No longer was there any doubt: we were also under arrest. We were too tired to stand any longer, so we crouched down on the ground, leaning against the gate.

Over an hour passed and still nothing happened.

While we were waiting, I felt myself starting to panic, and all kinds of gruesome scenes crowded into my mind: of women being beaten and mistreated and of dark underground prison cells. We prayed together quietly. That helped me to relax, and after a few minutes the images were gone.

DIANA THOMAS: Margrit had a two-way radio. We were all supposed to carry them for emergencies. One Talib tried to get the radio off me, but for some reason he didn't want to touch me—maybe because I was an infidel and unclean as a woman. I used that to my advantage and quickly put out a call, using code names.

'This is Delta Tango. Mike Sierra and I are in front of our office and the Tangos are taking us away——'

I got no further. One of our Afghan workers standing nearby said urgently, 'You'd better give it to him; he's getting angry.' So I handed the radio to the Talib.

Two people responded to my call. I could hear them but I couldn't talk to them.

❧

MARGRIT: The group of Taliban sitting about 20 metres away eyed us with disgust. Most were quite young, with dark sunburnt faces and black or white turbans. Some were wearing all black *shalwar kamiz*, others all white. (*Shalwar kamiz*, consisting of loose-fitting trousers and a long shirt, are the typical national dress of Afghanistan.)

One of the younger guys suddenly stood up and began walking towards us, playing menacingly with his Kalashnikov. 'Watch out, Margrit,' I heard an inner voice say. 'He's going to shoot at you, but he'll miss.'

'Thank you, Lord,' I whispered and quickly nudged Diana. 'Careful, he's going to shoot.'

Sure enough, the guy raised his Kalashnikov and aimed at us. The bullet whizzed just past our heads.

Diana and I ignored him. There was no way we were going to give him the satisfaction of seeing we were scared. We were furious at these guys for treating us this way, but at the same time grateful we had been prepared for this nerve-racking situation. Otherwise we would not have been able to react so calmly.

✧

PETER BUNCH: All the staff carried walkie-talkies which had a range of about three miles. I heard Diana's warning, grabbed our Afghan project manager, Gul Khan, and drove straight to the office. As we approached the building, we saw the group of Taliban standing there. Immediately we knew something was wrong.

'Drive on, quickly!' Gul Khan shouted at me.

I hit the accelerator. The Taliban were already running towards us. We could easily have escaped, but then I suddenly thought: *What about the women? I can't just leave them. They're in real difficulties. I have to help them!*

So I turned round and drove back to the Taliban.

The mob immediately encircled us, poking their Kalashnikovs through the side window. They grabbed my walkie-talkie and demanded I hand over the car keys. I resisted for as long as I could. But with guns pointing at us from almost every direction, it seemed I had little choice.

Then I tried to negotiate with them: 'What's this all about? Let the women go! They're just office staff.'

But there was no reasoning with them. They forced Margrit and Diana into the car along with as many guards as would fit. Then we drove ourselves to prison for interrogation.

✧

SILKE DUERRKOPF: I was suffering that weekend from gastric problems and had spent most of the time in bed. I had only been back in Afghanistan for a couple of days, having just had a ten-week break in Germany.

The frequent team meetings that weekend had proven hard going for me, so I took advantage of the lunch break to rest. I was woken by unusual sounds and voices. Every now and then I heard Kati's voice.

Something's not right here, I thought, and decided to get dressed.

I had just pulled my *shalwar kamiz* on when the door was ripped open and at least ten armed men marched into my bedroom.

This is outrageous, I thought indignantly. *I'm not even wearing a* chador! I felt incredibly ashamed and furious at the same time. By Western standards I was perfectly decent, but not according to Pashtun culture.

Talking in three languages at once, I shouted indignantly at the intruders, driving them out of the room and slamming the door in their faces. At that moment, I didn't care about the Kalashnikovs. All I wanted was a chance to dress myself properly.

Outside, Kati did her best to calm the men down and explain to them why I was so indignant. Amazingly, they did then allow me a few minutes. I threw my *chador* over my head and shoulders and walked out of the room.

The leader of the group asked me my name and whether I had anything to do with Shelter Now. They had clearly stumbled across me by accident and didn't even know who I was.

'You two come with us,' they ordered. 'We have some questions. It will only take one or two hours. Then you can go again.'

We followed them down the stairs. Suddenly I thought it would be good to take some money with me. I ran back into the room and stuffed my small linen bag containing a stack of dollar bills into my pocket. A Talib followed me quickly to see what I was up to, but fortunately he didn't appear to realise what was in the bag.

International bank transfers to Afghanistan are not easy, so I had brought a large amount of cash back with me from Germany. This money was to serve my fellow inmates and me well during the following months of imprisonment. Fortunately, no one showed any further interest in my bag during subsequent inspections.

'Okay,' I thought, 'I've only been back in Kabul a few days. This must be a huge misunderstanding.'

I was convinced that nothing would happen. The stamp in my passport was, after all, irrefutable proof that I had only just arrived in the country.

❧

GEORG: I was completely unaware of the arrests that had taken place on Sunday morning. While driving to our two o'clock meeting, I passed Kati and Silke's house and saw a group of Taliban hanging around.

'Strange,' I thought. 'What's going on here?'

I climbed out of the car to find out more. The group immediately charged over to me.

'Are you Mr George?'

'I'm Mr Taubmann,' I said. That immediately confused them and gave me time to think. 'What's going on?'

They grabbed hold of me roughly and dragged me into the house. There were Taliban everywhere. I was shocked, realising immediately that Kati and Silke must have been arrested too.

After a short conference among themselves, which I didn't understand, they snatched my car keys and dragged me over to my car, shoving me into the front passenger seat. A guard tried to squeeze in next to me but the door wouldn't close. They yanked me out again, tearing at my clothes, and then almost literally threw me into the back seat. Other Afghans rushing by looked on, dismayed and intimidated by the violent scene.

With me now wedged between two guards in the back seat, we sped off down the road. They took me to the Vice and Virtue Police headquarters, literally dragging me into the building by my clothes and treating me like a hardened criminal.

To suddenly be a prisoner is terrible. In their eyes, I no longer deserved any basic respect or esteem. When I had visited state institutions or offices in the past, I had always been respected as a foreigner, and in particular as the director of a reputable aid agency. But these people glared at me with disgust.

At some stage, I found myself sitting in a large office featuring a number of desks. Around fifteen Afghans were also in the room, some of them wild-looking young men. They gave me a form to fill out: name, age, name of father, name of grandfather, address, length of time in Afghani job description and so on. Then they fired questions at me.

'How many people are employed in your *madrassa* [religious school] and what are their names?'

'What? What do mean *madrassa*?' I couldn't understand what they were getting at. 'We don't have a *madrassa*. We don't even have any teachers. We just have a project in which we give boys work and something to eat.'

'No, no! That's not true. You will have to tell us how many teachers you have and what their names are,' they shouted.

There was nothing I could do to convince them.

The barrage of questions continued: 'How many projects do you have? Where are they? How many people have you employed? What are their names? Where do they live? Where are the other Americans?'

I was on my guard and named only those who I knew had already been arrested. I was desperate to protect the others if could. This first interrogation was very stressful, with questions fired at me nonstop.

Suddenly the door opened and Peter was brought in. Pleased to see me, he immediately tried to rush over to me but was held back.

'No talking!' someone bawled at us fiercely.

Peter was forced to sit on the floor on the other side of the room and fill out the same form.

ber of our Afghan employees were brought I was able to count eight in all: our ever-manager, engineers, drivers, a chef and they looked extremely dejected and fright-ank. I knew they would face far more brutal interrogation than we would. I couldn't bear to think about it. They were immediately led out past us and into another room.

⤚

PETER: When our car arrived at the religious police head-quarters, the women were led off one way and I was led into a room. It was filled with Afghans.

Then to my surprise I saw Georg at the other end of the room. He looked dejected and a bit wary, but not greatly afraid.

We weren't allowed to speak to one another, but it was a comfort to know that at least another person was there.

I had to fill out a form with all sorts of personal details. I don't know what my grandfather's name told them, especially since he was dead. Over the next few weeks we had to fill the same form out many times. I think they were looking for discrepancies, trying to get us to say things that would incriminate us.

⤚

When Georg had left the house at eleven o'clock that Sunday morning to go to the Foreign Ministry, Marianne and their two sons—sixteen-year-old Daniel and fourteen-year-old Benjamin—had stayed behind. Marianne busied herself with housework, but inside she was far from relaxed. She wondered whether the Taliban might decide to search their house too.

At around midday, she heard Diana's warning on the radio and was shocked to realise that two more of their staff were now evidently in trouble.

But where was Georg? She couldn't reach him by radio. She began to wonder whether he too had been arrested. The worry and uncertainty made her anxious and she started to ask around. No one could tell her anything.

After a while, one of Georg's longstanding Afghan friends came to the door. He held an influential position in one of the government ministries. 'Marianne,' he said, 'I have bad news. They've arrested Georg now as well.'

Although Marianne had already assumed as much herself, she was shaken by the certainty of the information. But she was able to pull herself together to respond.

'Ahmed Habib, I'll just quickly pack a bag with a few things. Could you make sure Georg gets it? All he has with him is what he's wearing.'

The man readily agreed, only too happy to help his friend.

A short while later, some of the other Shelter Now staff came by to offer Marianne comfort and to talk to the children to distract them. Preparing for the worst, Marianne began destroying any material she thought the religious police could take offence at. Other things which were important to her personally, including photos, holiday souvenirs and her favourite music CDs, she decided to bury in the garden.

Towards evening, Ahmed Habib returned. He was very upset.

'Marianne, the situation is very dangerous,' he said. 'You can't stay another night in this house. You have to leave. I've been told that the order to arrest your staff has come right from the top, from Mullah Omar himself. Come to my house for the time being; I will be able to protect you. You can stay with my wife and young son—you've yet to meet him anyway. Come and be our guest!'

Marianne thanked him for his kind invitation and told him that she and the children were preparing to leave the country the next day. She still had to pack and clarify a few things with the other foreign staff and asked him to return at 8.00 p.m. He said goodbye, and Marianne went to speak to the children in the living room.

'Come here and sit down with me,' she said to them and the friends who were still there. 'Things have become very serious. We won't be able to sleep here anymore and will have to leave Kabul very early in the morning.'

She phoned the remaining Shelter Now staff and arranged with them to meet at 4.00 a.m., ready to leave the city. To save space, each person was allowed to take just one suitcase.

Packing was a painful operation. There were far too many things that had become precious. One of the boys' suitcases was filled with school books alone so that only the other was left for personal things. They found it extremely difficult to part with their conglomeration of keepsakes and personal treasures.

Who knew whether they would ever see any of them again? Despite the shortage of space, their mother did allow one concession: the much-loved family guinea pig could not be left behind.

Marianne was not really afraid. She had lived through enough crises since being married to Georg to be able to keep a cool head in the situation. But it tore her apart to know that Georg was in prison and yet not to have any idea how he was getting on.

Eight o'clock that night came and went, but Ahmed Habib did not return. They waited an hour and then left the house for a safer location.

Early on Monday morning, all the remaining foreign staff of Shelter Now's Kabul team left the city in two cars, heading for Pakistan. There were eight adults and eight children. The journey to the border lasted around eight hours.

Along the way, they stopped off briefly at a public toilet, and Marianne suddenly spotted a familiar face. The man immediately came up to her and asked if she knew that twenty-four of their staff had now been arrested.

'So many? I only knew about eight,' she answered, shocked.

He quickly explained that he had just heard on Radio Sharia that a further sixteen of their Afghan employees had been taken into custody. Looking around warily, he added, 'Make sure you get out of here quickly before someone realises who you are!'

The team jumped back into their vehicles and drove

speedily to the border without any further stops. By the time they arrived it was lunchtime, and the guards on the Afghan side of the border were enjoying their meal. They simply stamped all the passports without looking too closely to see who the travellers were. The procedure on the Pakistani side was a little more complicated. Normally, everyone would have to leave the car, load their luggage onto a cart and then walk on foot to the Pakistani immigration office. But on that day, everything went very quickly. There was only one problem: an American family in the group did not have a valid visa for Pakistan.

The official in charge was unyielding. 'You'll have to go back to Kabul and apply for new visas,' he insisted.

Marianne summoned all her powers of persuasion. As she finally revealed that she was Georg's wife, the officer became a different man.

'Ah! Our Mr George!' he exclaimed.

Georg Taubmann was extremely popular and very respected in both countries. During his frequent border crossings, he always received priority treatment. The necessary visas were immediately issued, and the group soon found themselves safely on the Pakistani side.

From there they drove to Peshawar, where Shelter Now staff ran out to meet them, hugging them with relief.

৶

In Peshawar, Marianne heard from relatives of one of their Afghan house guards that their home in Kabul had been ransacked by Taliban that very same day.

After the liberation of Kabul, one of their friends went over to the house in the hope of recovering a few of their possessions. Most of the windows had been smashed, and soldiers from the Northern Alliance had also camped in the building. She was so shocked by the plundering and vandalism that at first all she could do was sit on the front doorstep and cry. She and her family had spent many happy hours in the Taubmann house.

The homes of the other Shelter Now workers suffered a similar fate. These people lost everything: clothes, furniture, kitchen and office equipment. That in itself was not easy. But it was the loss of personal things that was the most painful, things which in some cases had been treasured for a lifetime: books, CDs, photos, videos of birthdays and other special occasions, sea shells and minerals collected by the children, personal letters and drawings, notes and files stored on the computer.

Furniture and kitchen utensils can be replaced, but personal things are gone forever.

3

Behind Bars

After their arrest, the two Americans, Heather and Dayna, were immediately taken to the women's section of a Taliban reform school prison. There they joined around thirty Afghan women living in a small compound surrounded by high walls.

On Sunday afternoon, a day and a half later, they were unexpectedly joined by Silke and Kati.

SILKE: I still remember very clearly how Kati and I were led into the women's prison. It was a very strange kind of place.

First we were taken through a small gate which opened onto an inner courtyard. Then we had to climb through an opening in a wall where we were suddenly confronted by a huge building, with about twenty young Afghan boys peering at us from the windows. It was a *madrassa* run by the Vice and Virtue Police which doubled as a reform school for reluctant believers. As we later learned, this building was home to around 1500 boys and young men.

We stumbled down a narrow alleyway along the side of the building then followed our captors through a little wooden door into another small inner courtyard. It

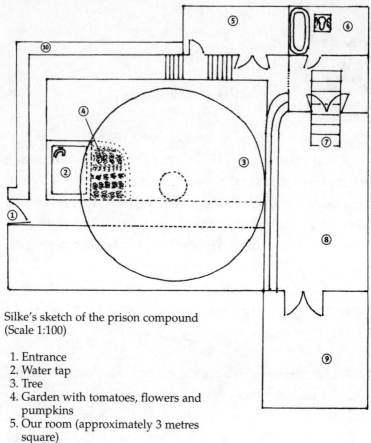

Silke's sketch of the prison compound
(Scale 1:100)

1. Entrance
2. Water tap
3. Tree
4. Garden with tomatoes, flowers and
   pumpkins
5. Our room (approximately 3 metres
   square)
6. Bathroom area
7. Steps to window
8. Stone platform
9. Room for Afghan women
   (approximately 4.5 metres square)
10. High wall

measured roughly 10 metres by 15 metres. In a flash we were
surrounded by Afghan women, mostly quite young. I began
to wonder what kind of place this was.

At the far end of the courtyard, two steps led up to a

stone platform. To the left of that was a wall with an open window. Rough stone steps led up to the window and down the other side to a kind of bathroom area. Getting to the bathroom without slipping over, particularly in the dark, turned out to be a challenge in itself.

There were two rooms adjoining the courtyard. One, about 4.5 metres square, was intended for the thirty Afghan women. A smaller one, about 3 metres square, I later discovered would be our room. Back near the door to the women's area was a freestanding tap where we could all get water. The yard itself was dominated by a huge tree, which offered welcome shade during those hot summer days.

❧

Silke and Kati were handed over to an older woman who was the overseer at the women's prison. After a short while, they caught sight of Dayna and Heather standing outside their room. Overjoyed at seeing them again, Silke and Kati charged over and hugged them profusely.

Evidently moved by this spontaneous outpouring of affection, the overseer left them alone for several minutes. But then she stepped in to separate them. She had strict orders not to allow the prisoners to talk to each other until their interrogation had been completed.

Some of the Afghan prisoners spread a blanket out under the tree in the yard, laid out a few cushions and served Silke and Kati tea. They all wore brightly coloured *shalwar kamiz* and plastic sandals. Some wore their long black or reddish hair tied up, others wore a plait. Some were extremely attractive and many were still only teenagers. All the women crowded round the German pair, fascinated by their every move. For Silke and Kati it was a bizarre feeling, rather like being exotic animals in a zoo.

They had just drunk a few sips of tea when the wooden gate opened again and Diana and Margrit were led in.

∾

DIANA: To get into the compound we had to bow through the door because it was quite low. We entered a courtyard filled with women and children.

Oh, is this someone's home? I wondered.

Then I noticed Silke and Kati sitting on the ground. *Oh no,* I thought, *they've got them too.*

I looked around. Off to one side was a little room, and I noticed Heather and Dayna standing at the door. That was amazing. That morning I had prayed, 'God, please let me see them today'—hoping they would come out, not expecting I would go in!

I ran up and embraced them, but the overseer separated us again.

∾

As they were not allowed to be with Heather and Dayna, the four women were taken to another building for the night. Their cell here was tiny, less than 3 metres square. The carpet was dirty and the air extremely bad. They had nothing that would serve as sheets to spread over the grimy mattresses. Their arrest had been so sudden that no one had brought anything with them. They just had to sleep in their clothes.

Silke soon felt panicked by the cramped conditions. She found herself fighting for air and realised she was suffering from claustrophobia. It looked as though she was about to collapse. Kati quickly grabbed her under the arms and took her outside the door where her breathing gradually returned to normal.

The guard ordered her to get back inside. When Silke failed to respond, he threatened to use his whip.

'My friend can't cope with it in there,' Kati tried to explain in her best Dari. 'She has claustrophobia. It's like an illness. Please take us somewhere else—we don't mind sleeping in the yard.'

The guard called the boss of the prison, who fortunately went along with their request. From then on, Silke and Kati slept on a mat in the yard, along with most of the Afghan women. The warm weather in August meant this was not a problem.

Meanwhile, Georg and Peter had been locked up in a prison cell at the Vice and Virtue Police headquarters. Their room was one normally used for men who had been whipped or jailed for a few days for not going to prayer or for wearing their hair or beard the wrong length. They had no idea where the women had been taken or what was happening to them.

✎

GEORG: When the Taliban showed us to a cell at the Vice and Virtue Police prison that first Sunday afternoon, we were initially in shock. Until that point I had never been in prison. I had heard other people talk about Afghan prisons, but I had never experienced them first-hand.

We were locked in a small room about 2.5 metres by 3 metres. There was no chair, no cupboard and no bed— just two thin, grimy mattresses on the floor. We had no pillows, no blankets and only the clothes we stood up in.

We flopped onto the mattresses and for a long time sat in silence. We were stupefied, unable to believe what was happening. The arrests had come like a bolt out of the blue.

It was hot inside the prison. The air was stuffy and stank of left over food. An army of flies seemed to close in on us, keen to investigate the new intruders.

After a while I stood up, trying to get my bearings in the semi-darkness. A naked bulb dangled from the ceiling, giving out a dingy light. In the wall opposite the door was a window, but it only looked into a kitchen where food was prepared for the Taliban. This was the source both of the revolting smell and of an incredible racket.

A second window, much smaller than the first, had a piece of rag hanging in front of it. Every now and then this would be pulled aside and an inquisitive Talib would peer in at us disapprovingly.

The walls were pitted with holes, the floor carpeted with dirt. I was extremely worried about the risk of vermin. It was not inconceivable that snakes or scorpions might find their way into our cell.

❧

PETER: The mattresses were infested with bed bugs. In the beginning, I thought they might have been mosquitoes. There were only bars on the windows, no glass or netting. But then huge welts came up all over my arms and legs. They were so itchy I could barely sleep.

Of course, Georg was bitten as well, but he wasn't affected anywhere near as much.

Trying to convince the Taliban that the problem was something other than mosquitoes was very difficult. It took us several days to find someone who would buy us the powder to dust the mattresses and some calamine lotion for the bites. Once we used those for a few days we were right.

❧

GEORG: It is terrible to be a prisoner. You sit, lie down, pace a few steps in one direction and a few back in the other. Basically you do nothing. Between the constant racket from the kitchen and our regular stream of peeping toms, even sleep was not a satisfactory option.

And then my thoughts returned to my team. Who had been arrested in the end? I knew about Heather and Dayna and some of our Afghan employees. But who else? How many of them, and how were they getting on?

And what about my wife and my two boys? Had the Taliban gone and searched our house? Were Marianne and the children locked up in these conditions somewhere too? The worry was unbearable.

I was grateful to have Peter with me and not to have

to face everything alone. His presence was a real comfort. Together we poured out our hearts to God. Our prayers reminded me of some of David's psalms of lament in the Bible.

∾

For the two men, the first night in prison was short. Georg dozed occasionally but found it hard to sleep properly in such surroundings. Peter, who never had a problem sleeping anywhere, fared a little better.

Just before 4.00 a.m., the first Taliban began shuffling past their cell to the bathroom area where they conducted their ceremonial washing. Right on four o'clock, the mullah's call to prayer rang out over the prison complex. The two prisoners looked forward to the end of morning prayers, when they hoped they would be left in peace for a few more hours.

But it was not to be. From then on, religious chanting droned from the *madrassa*. The noise and smell once again floated through from the kitchen, and every now and then a Talib would gape at them through the window.

At around seven o'clock they were given breakfast: *naan* bread and green tea.

Later that morning, the door was suddenly flung open and Gul Khan was pushed inside. Their loyal project manager looked pitiful. He hardly dared to look Georg in the face. He had been severely beaten up. The Taliban had sent him to fetch the keys for the Shelter Now office. Georg quickly handed them to the guard in the hope of sparing his project manager further suffering. At the same time, he realised bleakly that the Taliban were clearly not through with searching their premises.

As the guard left with Gul Khan, he casually handed Georg the bag which Marianne had asked Ahmed Habib to get to him.

∽

GEORG: That was a real surprise. I quickly unpacked it: there was a change of clothes, a handtowel, flannels for washing, soap, painkillers and sleeping tablets. And then the biggest prize of all: a bar of chocolate. I laid that to one side, deciding to save it in case it should come in useful later.

The memory of my family, and my worries and uncertainty about their well-being, suddenly overwhelmed me. Peter did his best to comfort me. And then, as if by coincidence, I felt inside one of the large pockets in the fresh *shalwar kamiz* and found a small note folded up.

'Dear Georg, I am in the care of good people and we are leaving for Pakistan.'

Overcome by emotion and relieved beyond belief, I clutched the note tightly, stammering, 'Thank you, Jesus. Thank you, Jesus.'

∽

Over the next few days, Georg refused to take any food. Using the little money he had left, he asked one of the guards to bring him bottled water from the market, but that was all.

'Mr George, why aren't you eating?' he was asked repeatedly.

Every time he would answer in a loud, complaining voice, 'Because this place is not fit for human habitation. Take us somewhere else. The smell from the kitchen, the heat, the noise, the darkness—it's intolerable! And why are we being held anyway? We haven't committed any crime. Let us go!'

But he was evidently complaining to the wrong people. Day after day they waited helplessly, with no news or information.

PETER: They didn't seem to understand that looking after us wasn't enough. That was the main thing that angered us. They would buy us cooked meals from the bazaar if we wanted them, so the problem wasn't that we weren't cared for. It was that they wouldn't tell us what was happening. And they wouldn't let us go.

We tried to explain. Even if they gave us hotel accommodation but didn't release us, we said, it would still be imprisonment. Either they didn't want to understand or couldn't. They seemed to think as long as we were not being mistreated, they could keep us as long as they wanted.

Over in the reform prison, the separation of Heather and Dayna from the other women continued. The religious police wanted to interrogate the two Americans before they had much contact with the others.

Altogether they were kept apart for a week and a half, then the six were together again.

MARGRIT: At first I thought we'd just be held for a few days and then released. At worst I thought we might get deported, as was common practice when the regime took a dislike to particular foreigners. There was nothing the Taliban could hold against me personally. I had just worked in the Shelter Now office.

The injustice of our situation and the realisation that we were totally at the mercy of the regime infuriated me. Then there was the terrible sense of isolation.

But there was no one we could complain to. No one would even tell us why we were being held or what crime we were supposed to have committed. We'd been ripped out of our everyday lives and locked up with nothing more than the clothes we stood up in.

KATI: After several days of imprisonment, after persistent asking, we were finally allowed to make a brief visit to our houses. When I entered our house, I was appalled at what I found. My carefully crafted photo board with pictures of family and friends had been ripped off the wall, the photos shredded into tiny pieces and thrown all over the floor. Many things were missing.

I turned on the Taliban guards, shouting at them in fury. But they just made fun of me and told me to be quick.

It is very humiliating trying to pack underwear and

other personal things while ten men with Kalashnikovs are looking over your shoulder impatiently. I was hardly able to think straight, and as a result ended up forgetting half the things I wanted. In any case, I thought it would only be for a few days and then I'd be home again.

❧

SILKE: The guards checked everything before we packed it in a bag and wouldn't let us take everything. We weren't all allowed to take a Bible, for example. And they allowed hardly any card games or books.

'You won't need that much. You'll be free in no time,' they claimed.

I quickly packed two changes of *shalwar kamiz*, my glasses, a few books, medicines, soap and shampoo. Little did I realise that, apart from a few things we received later from the foreign embassies, these items were all I would have for the next three months.

❧

DIANA: They took us at about 9.30 in the evening—they always did things at night. Even their cars were heavily tinted so no one could see in.

The trip was awful. We were bundled into two cars packed with Taliban. It was pathetic—all those men with Kalashnikovs to guard six vulnerable women. As we drove they pretended they didn't know where we lived. But I watched the driver, and he knew exactly where to turn even before we told him.

They had already broken into our homes and people

were already living there. In one house family photos had been ripped up and in another all our CDs had been confiscated (music and photos were banned by the Taliban). We had quite a hair-raising night.

Peter and Georg didn't go back to their homes. Georg couldn't be 100 per cent sure his wife and children had got away, and Peter had been living with an American family and didn't want to risk endangering them. So Peter wore the same *shalwar kamiz* for three weeks.

∞

Once they were back together, the six women developed a daily routine, being careful to retain some self-discipline so that they were not tempted to just let themselves go.

∞

KATI: For Afghans, the day begins at 4.00 a.m. The prison compound had its own minaret, and every morning the mullah would sing from his tower, his voice amplified many times over by a deafening system of loudspeakers. Even with three blankets wrapped tightly over my head, it was impossible to sleep through it.

Immediately the Afghan women would be up and bustling around, attending to their ceremonial washing, sweeping the courtyard and saying their prayers. As Kati and I were sleeping outside, we had to watch out not to get swept up with the dust. The night was over.

By about 6.00 a.m. everyone had showered and was ready for the day. The 'shower' was a watering can of cold water which we poured over each other. At about 7.00 breakfast would arrive, consisting of *naan* bread and tea. From 7.30 until midday, the Afghan women received instruction in their room. They were there for the purposes of 're-education' and received intensive teaching in the principles of Islam Taliban-style.

For us this time was golden—the only chance for a bit of peace and quiet. With just under forty women living in a small yard, there was always plenty going on. During these precious hours of respite, we would spread out, each to a different corner of the yard. We might read or write something, reflect on things or pray. Sometimes someone would sing something quietly to herself—three of us in fact composed a number of songs while in prison and then taught them to the others.

Every morning at about 9.30, we would get together and each one would talk about how she was doing. We would read from the Bible, pray and encourage each other. This time usually lasted until the other women returned around midday.

The afternoons were usually pretty quiet. Daytime in Kabul in August and September is still very hot. Most people found a place in the shade and dozed off. From around 5.00 p.m. life gradually returned to the yard. Some of the Afghan women took a shower or treated their hair with various forms of mud pack. Others started sweeping the yard again (one of the chief occupations in the prison) and spreading out their mattresses ready for the night. The evening meal was very irregular: sometimes it would come early, other times very late.

When darkness fell—about seven o'clock in August—most of the women lay down to go to sleep. We could do very little else. A single light bulb hung from the tree, glowing pathetically. The light in the bathroom didn't usually work at all, turning any nightly trip to the squat toilet into a risky escapade. The concrete steps up to the window opening in the wall were steep and irregular; you then had to duck your head sharply to get through the gap, and getting down the other side was an equally precarious operation. In the darkness it was difficult to hit the hole accurately, so invariably there was as much excrement beside the toilet as in it—a particularly evil last hurdle on the nightly assault course.

᭰

DIANA: The toilet was really just a hole. It was particularly miserable because we started suffering dysentery from drinking the untreated water. If you needed to go to the toilet and someone was already in there, sometimes you just didn't make it.

Having a routine really helped us get through the day. We found different ways to pass the time. At one stage some of the girls were competing to kill 200 flies each day. They would line them up and count them.

We didn't have just flies. We had scorpions. We had mice. We watched the Afghan women picking head lice out of each other's hair, and before long two of us had head lice too. We were able to order treatments from the chemist to deal with things like that. Someone would buy them for us if we gave them the money.

As a nurse I found I had a lot of health needs to attend to. It wasn't just our girls; the prisoners were often ill. They couldn't afford even basic pain killers, so we started ordering medicines for them and praying for them.

One day Dayna fell very heavily on her rib cage. She was in great pain and started getting very tight in her chest at night. I didn't know how to help her.

'Lord, what am I going to do?' I prayed desperately.

One morning I woke up with the name of a particular drug on my mind. 'You know,' I said to Dayna, 'I think God wants us to start you on this drug.' So I ordered it and we tried it out, and Dayna's breathing at night improved.

Many times I had to cry out to God like that because I didn't know what else to do.

✢

KATI: We soon started to get to know the other Afghan women better and developed a real respect for them. They also began to trust us more, perhaps because we made such an effort to fit in with their culture. We were careful to wear *chadors* at all times. And washing dishes while holding on to your *chador* is no mean feat!

The women were also extremely helpful. They always wanted to wash our clothes for us, for instance. But I didn't want that and asked them to show me how to do it instead. They showed us how to rub the clothes together and then beat them as thoroughly as possible so that creases didn't develop.

✢

MARGRIT: Out of solidarity with the Afghan women, whom we increasingly came to love and respect, we decided to stick to the simple prison diet.

In the mornings, we were given *naan* bread and green tea. At midday and in the evening we had vegetables—usually pumpkin, beans or eggplant, occasionally with potatoes or rice. Only one vegetable at a time, though, never a mixture. Now and then we were treated to 'dog food' (as we called it). This carnivorous concoction consisted mainly of bones and fat boiled in water. In the middle of the colourless, unseasoned soup would be floating one small scrap of meat—supposedly enough for six people. Fortunately it did come with bread, which was at least more effective in staving off the hunger pangs.

The food was served in metal bowls. One bowl filled with just about two fingers worth of food was supposed to serve two to three people. It was really not very much, and the meals became fewer as time progressed.

In Afghanistan, the families of prisoners are responsible for ensuring there is enough food which means they end up bringing food into the prison each day—if they're able to. Those without families go hungry. We fell in line with the other Afghan women and only asked the guards to buy us things from the market which the other prisoners received from their relatives, such as tomatoes, cucumbers and carrots. Eventually we got bottled water and basic medicines as well.

We did, of course, try to sneak some of these things to the poorer women who didn't receive regular food from relatives. But we were often prevented from doing so.

❧

KATI: Because I can speak a little of both Dari and Pashtu, I was able to have quite detailed conversations with the women and ask why they had been locked up.

One woman was there because she had opened her front door without donning a *burka* first as the law dictated.

One of the girls was just twelve years old. She was married and had run away from her husband because he beat her. In fact, a large number of women were there because they had fled from violent husbands. We were told that a lot of teenage women were sent to the prison because they refused to marry Taliban or because their families were unable to pay the dowry.

As a rule, the search for a bride proceeded roughly as follows. If a Talib took a fancy to a particular young girl and wanted to marry her (even though, with the *burka*, there wasn't much of her to see!), he would give the family an ultimatum: either they hand over the daughter for marriage or pay the Talib compensation. This 'compensation' was generally some astronomical sum which the family would never be able to afford. If things didn't proceed to the Talib's satisfaction, the girl suddenly found herself locked up at the reform school.

Another of the women we knew already. She had often visited us at home and secretly sold us very attractive pieces of embroidery. Her husband disapproved of her selling things to us; as a woman, she was not supposed to engage in any kind of trade. He also disapproved of us living in a house alone as women, with no male relatives. Unfortunately, she came by our house again after we'd been arrested and was promptly seized by the Taliban, who were still there. They immediately packed her off to the reform school.

The worst thing was, she had a two-year-old daughter at home and didn't know whether anyone would look after her there. I appealed to the guards passionately on her behalf, and two days later her daughter was brought to her in the prison.

Yet another woman had been locked up, together with her mother, because the two of them had been caught selling eggs on the street. She was in total despair because she had left her two children, two and four years old, locked in at home without food or water. Rarely have I heard anyone wail like this woman did—the whole night.

Again we did all we could, scolding, threatening and begging the guards on her behalf. Finally—miracle of miracles! —they let her go so she could return to her children.

There were two other girls we knew from our district. They had been caught trying to sell fruit and vegetables from a wooden barrel while dressed up as boys. They, like all the rest of the women, had been sent to the reform school to learn to be good Muslims through physical punishment and strict teaching from the Koran.

The Taliban's Declaration of War on Women

The rise to power of the Islamic fundamentalists in 1992 saw a new chapter in the history of oppression of Afghanistan's women. Relatively advanced laws relating to women were immediately rescinded. A *fatwah* (general legal report based on the *sharia* law) cited the education of women as a source of seduction and depravity.

At the same time, it was also decided that there was no necessity for women to leave the house for the purpose of purchasing items of any nature. Only if she first fulfilled sixteen conditions (which applied primarily to her dress and behaviour) could a woman leave the house at all. These conditions included obtaining permission from her husband and having a male relative to chaperone her. While out on the street, she was forbidden to look at any strangers and could only talk with them if absolutely necessary.

Under the rule of the Taliban from the mid-1990s, the *fatwah* became even more rigorous. From then on, women were only allowed to leave the house if every part of their body was covered by the *burka*. Suddenly there were no limits to the tyranny.

One eighteen-year-old woman whose head covering had allegedly slipped a little was kicked into the river by a Taliban fighter, where she drowned. A girl who was found to be wearing red nail polish had one finger of her right hand chopped off with an axe.

Women could no longer be treated in the general hospitals, which meant they had little or no access to medical care. For women with no husbands—widows or unmarried women—the rules of the Taliban became a deadly snare. Every means of living was denied them: they possessed no income, had no breadwinner and were not even allowed to leave the house to go shopping. Many of these women faced starvation.

MARGRIT: Violence was a part of everyday life in the women's prison. Our overseer always carried a piece of plastic pipe which she used when she intervened in disputes between the women. Often we didn't even know what the dispute was about; we only heard the blows and saw her beating the women with her pipe.

The girls could easily cope with one or two blows. But when they sat on the floor cowering and she kept on beating them, we couldn't bear it anymore and intervened. Then she usually stopped. She wasn't actually a particularly violent woman, but slaps and beatings seemed to be a normal part of life for women in Afghan culture.

The story of one of these women touched me deeply. She was roughly the same age as me and a really sweet person. Very attractive, with reddish hair and a gentle nature, she also seemed to be a little better educated and more mature than the others. Unfortunately, she could only speak Dari and I could only speak Pashtu, but we often exchanged friendly glances and tried to communicate using sign language.

On a number of occasions, the guards would come to collect her late in the evening or in the morning. One morning I saw her hobbling painfully into the yard. She flopped onto her mattress, pulled the cover over her head and lay there motionless for the rest of the day. I learned that she had refused to pray in the exact way prescribed by the rules and had therefore been beaten with a leather whip on the soles of her feet. Over the next few days, she was barely able to walk. She seemed completely apathetic and broken. It took a whole week before she was up and moving round normally again.

I found it terrible to see her lying there day after day. It affected me a great deal to see this gentle, attractive woman so devastated.

❧

KATI: At the beginning, we were allowed to sit together with the Afghan women, chat with them and drink tea. Later we were barred from such contact. But if our overseer was in a good mood, she would sometimes allow us to talk to them.

Afghan women are known for their hospitality and friendly nature. One day, two women who were drinking tea together invited Heather—who just happened to be walking past—to join them. Heather turned to ask permission from the warder, who appeared not to object. Although they only sat together for five minutes, as soon as Heather left them the warder came and took the two women to their room where she beat them. She put mattresses against the door to block out the sound, but for a whole thirty minutes we could hear the muffled screams as the women were beaten.

This was a terrible experience for all of us, especially because we felt it was our fault they were punished.

❧

SILKE: One evening I was standing at the water tap in the yard cleaning my teeth. Suddenly I realised that something was wrong—the women around me had frozen to the spot. A hideous sound was coming from the other side of the wall: the lashing of a whip accompanied by grotesque laughter.

A group of men—there must have been about fifty of them—were laughing raucously and making jokes. I could clearly distinguish the voice of our top prison director. They were evidently whipping two young men. Never in my life have I heard men scream like those two did. The whole thing lasted about three quarters of an hour. Afterwards, one of the victims was forced to sing something while the men made fun of him. I couldn't help but think of the Gestapo. It all seemed so demonic.

Throughout this incident, I sat on the floor with the other women and wept silently. Others stood around motionlessly, their eyes wide with fear. It was so quiet on our side of the wall you could have heard a pin drop. Everyone shared in the suffering of those two men.

But in spite of all the humiliations and the unceasing brutality which was part and parcel of their lives, the Afghan women exhibited an incredibly strong, unbroken will to live. They were mistreated and downtrodden, but no one could rob them of their inner freedom.

One example was music—strictly forbidden under the Taliban. When our overseer went out, the women would take their washing bowls, turn them upside down and quietly drum on them with the tips of their fingers and the balls of their hands. They had an incredible sense of rhythm. They could conjure up fascinating sequences which they would then dance to, taking very small steps. Each woman had her own unique type of dance through which she expressed herself.

It was their way of protesting. I realised the Taliban would never manage to break the life and energy of these brave women. I felt such a love for them.

One woman was an especially gifted comedian. Once she wound a piece of cloth round her head like a turban, painted a beard on her face using charcoal from a cooking pot and donned a black *shalwar kamiz*. Her Talib costume complete, she proceeded to do everything that was strictly forbidden in Afghanistan. She filmed the girls with an imaginary camera. She blew wolf-whistles at them. She acted out a pair of lovers, holding hands with her partner and giving him kisses. In all this, she imitated perfectly the boorish behaviour of a Talib.

It was first-class entertainment and got everyone laughing.

4

Interrogation

For Georg and Peter, the initial days spent at the head-quarters of the religious police were full of uncertainty, boredom and worrying questions about the immediate future. But when Friday morning of their first week in captivity came, everything started happening at once.

'Out, out, out!' the guard shouted at Georg. 'Get your things and follow me!'

One of the Taliban's tactics for intimidating their prisoners was to suddenly confront them with new situations without warning and demand speed at the same time.

Peter stared after Georg's retreating figure, puzzled. He was left in the cell alone.

'Where are we going?' asked Georg with concern. 'Why can't Peter come too?'

Without answering or offering any other information, the guards led Georg to his first interrogation session. It lasted from that morning until late into the night. This session was held at another prison, and once it was over, the men couldn't be bothered driving him back to the Vice and Virtue prison. So they parked him in a cell to sleep for a few hours before waking him early next morning for more questioning.

Unbeknown to Georg, he was now in the same reform school prison as the six women, and his new cell was the room where Diana, Silke, Margrit and Kati had stayed until they were reunited with Dayna and Heather.

For Georg the cell was just as small as the one at the Vice and Virtue headquarters, but a little more comfortable. It was not quite so dirty, and there was a lot less noise, not to mention the welcome absence of kitchen odours. But once again, there were only two thin mattresses on the floor and no furniture at all.

A cupboard on the wall belonged to the guards, which meant they were forever coming in to fetch something. A window located on the northern side of the cell looked directly onto a wall, so Georg never saw the sun. The door was not locked, which meant he could walk to the bathroom adjoining his cell without having to ask a guard. But there was always someone watching in the corridor.

Georg spent three days alone in this cell, between interrogation sessions, before Peter was finally brought to join him, bringing a welcome end to his forced solitude.

❧

PETER: I was quite shocked when they came and fetched poor Georg from our cell that Friday morning. When the whole day went by without him returning, I started to feel anxious. Apart from anything else, I'd got used to being with him—and to then suddenly find myself alone was rather scary.

'Where's Georg?' I asked the guard outside my door. 'What have you done with him?' But I got no answer.

The whole night passed without him returning. This was followed by another two days. By this time I was really worried.

I kept thinking: *Maybe they're actually torturing him, or maybe I won't ever see him again.* I couldn't bear it. I started to pray my heart out for him.

And then something quite unexpected happened. I was using the bathroom when a group of Taliban started hammering on the door like madmen. 'Get moving! Come out here immediately! We're taking you somewhere else!'

For three and a half days they had let me stew without a scrap of information. Now, just because it took their fancy, I was supposed to stop what I was doing and spring to attention. I laughed at them and purposely took longer than I needed.

They were mad at me as a result, but they took me to another prison without further incident. There I was finally reunited with Georg. He was sitting in front of his cell as cool as you please, chatting to some of the guards.

'I'm fine, Peter, don't worry,' he greeted me. 'This cell is better than the other one and the guys here are nicer too.'

I had my own thoughts as regards the 'better' treatment. But the main thing was that I was back with my friend. Nothing else really mattered.

❧

Georg's interrogators—four or five men in total—took it in turns to grill him. Two of them had clearly received some form of training for the job. One who was particularly aggressive was later nicknamed 'Long Nose' by the two prisoners. Occasionally, when the interrogators were addressing religious issues, they were joined by the mullah from the neighbouring *madrassa*.

Owing to the various languages involved and the complicated procedure adopted, the interrogation was an extremely long-winded affair. First of all, a translator had to write down the interrogator's question in English. Georg then answered in English, and his answer was translated orally into Pashtu. Afterwards Georg had to write down his own answer in English and then date and sign it.

※

GEORG: This business of signing statements was very critical for me. The proceedings were incredibly demanding on my concentration. I had to be extremely careful how I answered, particularly with questions which were repeated again and again. They were forever trying to get me to confess to things I hadn't done by repeating false accusations.

After every question and answer session I was totally exhausted. The longer these sessions lasted (one continued for sixteen hours without a break), the harder it was to keep my concentration.

At the beginning, my interrogators were reasonably pleasant. But their mood and their mode of questioning could switch very suddenly. Some sessions were very aggressive and frightening. I was totally at their mercy. I was never beaten physically, but they often laid into me verbally.

To begin with, most of the questioning related to the aid organisation: what projects we were running, how many foreign workers we had, how many Afghans we employed. They demanded to know exactly where all our houses were and how far in advance we had paid the rent. They even wanted to see our rent contracts.

What Georg did not know was that the Taliban had already impounded their houses, and a short while later had cleaned them out of anything worth having before vandalising what was left. All their office equipment and computers, along with Shelter Now's fleet of vehicles, had been taken for the service of the Taliban. This occurred even before the suspects were questioned, let alone a court ruling passed.

At the same time, factories run by Shelter Now in other provinces of Afghanistan, which produced prefabricated concrete building materials, were also destroyed and the Afghan staff harassed.

The Vice and Virtue Police were evidently quite sure that their prisoners would sign everything under pressure, allowing them to annex the organisation's private property. Otherwise they would undoubtedly not have acted so prematurely.

GEORG: Our children's project turned out to be a particularly critical issue. The Taliban claimed we had run it illegally and had secretly set up a *madrassa* to teach the children about Christianity.

In fact, we had discussed everything with the government planning office beforehand and obtained permission prior to starting up the project. But out of fear of the religious police, staff at the planning office suddenly decided they knew nothing about us. Interestingly, the permit itself also disappeared.

At every opportunity, the Taliban would suddenly interrupt their line of questioning with: 'And how many teachers do you have? What are their names? Where do they live?' But I never tired of giving the same honest answer: 'We haven't been working illegally. We had a permit. We don't have a *madrassa*, and we don't have any teachers. We never taught the children anything. We only gave them food plus an hour's work a day so that they could earn a little money.'

'No, no, no! That's not true. We have information that Christian teaching was also given there. You as director must be aware of these things.'

It was all lies from beginning to end, but they used every means at their disposal to try to draw a confession from me.

Another accusation was that we'd engaged in Christian proselytising. The fact that the two women had shown the documentary film about Jesus came as welcome evidence to support their case. During this session, the mullah from next door was present.

'As director, you are responsible for everything!' they shouted at me menacingly. 'In our country, it is a criminal act to show such a film.'

'I cannot be held responsible for everything that my staff do in their free time,' I said. 'In any case, this film has been broadcast on television in many Muslim countries. Lots of Muslims in Pakistan have watched this film. Even you believe that Jesus is a great prophet.'

'But you persuaded Muslims in Afghanistan to become Christians,' they said.

'Afghans often talk about religion,' I countered. 'They ask us what we believe and so we tell them that we're Christians. Is it not permitted to talk about religion in your country?'

'Of course. But you use your aid projects as a bait and turn the refugees in your camps into Christians.'

'That's not true,' I repeated. 'Shelter Now is an aid organisation. We build houses, dig wells and ensure that food is distributed fairly. We help anyone no matter what religion they are, and we ask nothing in return.'

'No, we have evidence against you. We've found a lot of Christian literature and Bibles in your houses.'

'Then show me,' I challenged, knowing full well that they could have found no such thing.

Long Nose suddenly became very aggressive. 'You're a bunch of criminals!' he screamed at me.

That was too much. Now it was my turn to start shouting. 'A criminal is someone who robs others or kills people, not someone who shows a documentary film about Jesus! Go to our camps where for many years we've been providing food for your Afghan refugees. Take a look at the camps in Pakistan. Ask the Afghans who know us in Kandahar, in Helmand, Khost and Logar and have seen our projects there. Go and ask them what they think of us. They respect us and are deeply grateful for all the help we've given them. I find it a grave insult to be called a criminal!'

To that they had no answer. They looked a little awkward and immediately broke off the interrogation.

These sessions followed the same pattern daily for two weeks. It was a very difficult time. I asked Peter to pray for me while I was away. Decisive footsteps in the corridor were enough to make me flinch inwardly. Fear would come over me: 'Here we go again.'

The Islamic Understanding of Missions

The selfless, neighbourly love and practical help that the Bible encourages Christians to practise without respect to race or religion can easily be misinterpreted by some Muslims. The accusation of 'proselytising' was linked with the assumption that the assistance provided by Shelter Now could only be given in return for something.

This approach has been used by some Christians and is a common form of mission in Islam. It has happened in animist villages in some rural areas in Asia, for example, where electricity has been brought, roads and schools have been built, and wells have been dug—but only when the villagers have agreed to become Muslims.

The Shelter Now workers were accused of adopting the same method. It proved impossible to disabuse the Taliban of this idea.

PETER: My own interrogation began as soon as I was transferred to the new cell. But it was not nearly as bad as Georg's. He was questioned for many sessions lasting several hours each, but I only faced about five hours of questioning in total. I was able to get through it reasonably easily.

In the end, I had nothing to be afraid of—I knew they didn't have anything against me personally. They were welcome to search my house as well. I knew that however hard they tried, they would not find anything remotely suspicious there. What could they accuse an engineer of anyway?

Obviously, during the interrogation they ran our female colleagues down and accused me of things which quite simply weren't true. But it was very easy to see through their lies. Their tactics weren't exactly clever. And sure enough, it didn't take long before they gave up on me.

But they still didn't release me.

While the two men were being questioned in one part of the reform school, the women were undergoing continuing interrogation in the women's section next door. Neither group was aware the other was nearby.

KATI: When we later heard from Georg how he was really put through the mill during his interrogation by the Taliban, we realised we'd had things relatively easy.

Heather, Dayna and I were asked the most questions. These revolved largely around the visit to the Afghan family and the children's project. I didn't find the interrogation that bad, but I tend to be someone who sees things positively.

My biggest worry was that I might incriminate others unwittingly by not expressing myself absolutely correctly when it came to the controversial issues. Before giving every answer, I prayed silently that the right things would occur to me—and in the end everything went okay.

❧

DIANA: As I'd worked for Shelter Now for over eight years, my interrogators asked me detailed questions about the organisation. What else could they ask me? I was completely innocent—unless my work there as a secretary could be seen as a reason for my arrest.

Obviously they tried to pin things on me. One time they said they had found 'radio cards' in our offices. These cards were basically pieces of notepaper with the frequencies of forbidden radio stations written on them. For the Taliban, such cards were devilish.

'Tell me in which room you found the cards and I'll tell you who they belong to,' I answered.

But of course they couldn't tell me. When I later read the charges against me, I noticed they still mentioned that these radio cards had been found in my possession, even though during my interrogation I stated clearly that I did not possess any such cards and signed a statement accordingly.

They asked me three times why I wasn't married. In the end, I told them flatly, 'I have a good job, a car, a house.

Why do I need a husband?' They never mentioned that subject again.

The translator was a very kind man. Whenever he led one of us out of the office to collect the next one, he would leave us in the little room outside for a short while so that we could quickly exchange notes on what we'd been asked and how we'd answered. In this way it was possible to ensure that our answers tallied even in the minor details.

SILKE: On the first evening of our interrogation they fetched us at around 7.00 p.m. and we were interrogated until midnight. The questions always seemed to be incredibly stupid and very uncoordinated. Up to seven men sat in front of us posing the questions—there were always new Taliban joining the group. There was a translator too.

They repeatedly asked the same things. I must have given my father's name, grandfather's name, place of birth and so on at least twenty times. Each time, everything had to be translated, making it a very long and tedious process.

On that first night, I felt it wasn't right that we women had to sit with strange men in a room until midnight— particularly as this was the famous Vice and Virtue Police, who ought to know the social manners in their country. On the second day, as I was sitting there once again late in the evening, I felt really mad about it.

'Why do you look so dejected?' I was asked. 'There would be no reason for you to look like that if you were innocent as you claim.'

I answered calmly and politely. 'I am very disappointed

by the way we, as women, are being treated here. We have
made every effort to fit in with your culture. We dress and
behave like Afghan women. It's hardly surprising that we
then feel dishonoured when we are forced to sit in a room
alone with men in the middle of the night. It brings shame
on us. Judge for yourselves whether it's right or not.' Then
I added in a more conciliatory tone, 'I would be happy to
answer your questions during the day and in the presence of
another woman.'

All the men immediately jumped up and left the room.
After a short while, the translator returned with the prison
director and both of them apologised to me. 'We understand your feelings,' they said. 'This won't happen again.'

From then on, all our interrogation sessions took place
during the day, and an Afghan female guard was ordered to
attend and watch over our honour.

MARGRIT: All of us were basically asked the same questions.
When it was my turn, my interrogators tried to say I'd been
involved in working at the children's project too. I told
them repeatedly that I had only ever worked in the office
and was not involved in any of Shelter's projects. This was
the truth. I wrote the same thing in English for the official
record and signed it.

We were also informed that as soon as the investigations
were complete, we would be released from prison and
simply deported from Afghanistan. So we were told not to
worry.

When I later read the charges against me, I was amazed

to see that they included my alleged involvement in the children's project, despite my persistent denials. I couldn't believe it. It should have been obvious that I and several of the others ought to have been released as soon as our interrogation was over.

One of the Taliban interrogating me asked right at the beginning of our imprisonment why I was fasting. Muslims are only familiar with the fasting month of Ramadan, during which they neither eat nor drink from sunrise to sunset.

'My fasting is not a form of hunger strike,' I said. 'I don't wish to offend anyone by it. For me, fasting is a sacrifice to God and it strengthens me in prayer.'

I then went on to explain what prayer and worship meant for me.

'Prayer is not a ritual as far as I'm concerned, but simply talking to God—being honest with him about the things I'm thinking and feeling. God isn't distant; he's very close to me. I have a personal relationship with him, and sometimes I sense him saying things to me and giving me peace and strength.'

✦

For the women, life in the prison dragged. The hope of release soon gave way to the worrying question of what kind of game the Taliban were playing—and why.

After a week or so, the appalling sanitary conditions began to take their toll. Dayna suffered from asthma. Silke went down with bronchitis because the nights outside grew cooler and the blankets were too thin. The women fought with bed bugs, lice and worms. All of them suffered from gastric problems.

They found the total isolation from the outside world particularly tough. They were not allowed to write or receive any letters. The Taliban were free to do with them as they pleased, and no one was able to intervene.

They also wondered what was going on outside and what was being done to secure their release. They had no idea that people all over the world, from all sorts of different churches, were praying for them. Nor did they realise that their cause was front page news in Germany, Australia, the United States and many other countries.

The Shelter Now staff in Peshawar exhausted every avenue they could think of trying to persuade the Pakistani government to intervene. Back in Germany, where Shelter Now's European office is based, staff were in constant contact with the German Foreign Ministry and did all they could to keep the plight of the aid workers in the public eye. At times the chairman, Udo Stolte, and his deputy, Joachim Jaeger, gave up to forty interviews a day to press organisations from around the world.

In Australia and the United States political leaders expressed grave concern. The Australian Department of Foreign Affairs and Trade kept in daily contact with Diana's and Peter's relatives. In Pakistan the German embassy demanded the release of the aid workers, and Australian and US diplomats insisted on getting access to the prisoners. But the Taliban refused to allow

A few days before his arrest, Georg is still able to carry out his work freely.

The Shelter Now aid workers before Afghanistan's Supreme Court.
ZDF

Above: Georg takes an opportunity to tell the press that all the aid workers are well.
REUTERS

Right: The appalling sanitary conditions in a Kabul prison.

Georg and Peter in their cell.

Georg with one of the inmates.

The pictures on these two pages were taken with a camera that was smuggled into the prison.

Making tea in the prison was a risky operation.

The six Shelter Now women in prison, wearing traditional *burkas*.

The six Shelter Now women in prison with their *burkas* pushed back.

Silke sitting on her mattress in the women's prison.

Shipping containers like these were frequently used as prisons or places of execution during the Afghan civil war.

The eight hostages after their release from the prison in Ghazni.

At the International Red Cross office in Ghazni.

Georg and Marianne are reunited at Frankfurt airport after more than three months of separation.

The eight hostages after their rescue (left to right): Peter Bunch, Dayna Curry, Margrit Stebner, Georg Taubmann, Heather Mercer, Silke Duerrkopf, Katrin Jelinek, Diana Thomas.

The three women from Germany attending a reception arranged by the mayor of their home city, Braunschweig.

any diplomatic representatives entry into Afghanistan. Even the International Committee of the Red Cross was not allowed to examine or see the aid workers.

Meanwhile, Heather's father and Dayna's mother flew to Islamabad and were waiting in trepidation for permission to enter Afghanistan.

When the Western diplomats and the two parents were finally allowed to fly to Kabul on 13 August, they were then refused permission to visit the prison. They tried persistently to negotiate with the Foreign Ministry in Kabul, but to no avail. When their visas ran out, they were forced to leave empty-handed. It was a clear humiliation for the West.

Finally, on Sunday 26 August, exactly three weeks after the aid workers' arrest, they received their first visitors: a five-strong delegation from the ICRC. The prison director, however, would not allow the delegation to speak to the men and women together at the same time.

The women fought this decision tooth and nail. 'We'll only talk with the delegation if the men are allowed to attend too,' argued Diana, fighting doggedly for a reunion with Georg and Peter. 'Our boss told us that we shouldn't speak to a delegation in his absence.'

After a long tug-of-war, all eight prisoners were allowed to see each other briefly—although only in the presence of Taliban guards.

⋙

DIANA: Words cannot describe how good it was to finally see Georg and Peter again and to know they were unharmed. For three weeks we had been denied all contact. We knew right from the beginning that Peter had been detained, but it wasn't until much later that we learned about Georg's arrest from a guard.

During this first meeting we were all quite emotional. We were overjoyed to see each other and everyone talked at once.

The doctors asked whether we were being treated well and told us we could write letters to family and friends which they would pass on. Of course, we wrote as soon as the visit was over, but unfortunately our letters never left the prison. They were immediately destroyed by the Taliban.

The brief half hour that we were allowed to spend together flew by. Then the men were led away to be examined by the doctors and we women were examined by a nurse. We showed the women delegates the prison toilet and they wrote down details about our living conditions. They left us some medication and gave us a few medical tips for life in prison.

They promised to come back, but of course the Taliban wouldn't let them.

❧

GEORG: I had managed to befriend several of our guards, and now and again they would pass on news to me that they heard on the radio. So I was aware that our diplomats had made great efforts to get to Kabul but hadn't been permitted to see us because the Taliban were not yet through with our interrogation. One indicator that something was likely to happen soon came the day before the visit. The guards suddenly started cleaning and smartening up all the rooms and corridors.

The next day, Peter and I were taken to the prison director's office where we saw our six colleagues for the first time since our arrest. I was so moved I could not hold back the tears.

During the conversation that followed, the doctors only asked a few questions. It was obvious they could not say much because of the presence of the guards.

'We're not allowed to talk to you about political matters,' they told us. 'But we want to know how you are doing and give you an all-round medical check-up. That is our mandate.'

The doctors later went with Peter and myself to another room for examination. There they asked to be able to speak to us alone.

'We can't allow that,' said the director. 'One of the guards will remain present.'

'But it's our right,' argued one of the doctors. 'We are allowed to talk to the prisoners without witnesses. That's the way things are done in all countries.'

Reluctantly, the English-speaking Talib went outside, only to return a few moments later.

In this short time, the doctors quickly asked, 'How are you really doing? Have you really not been mistreated in any way? Do you have anything else important to tell us?'

❧

PETER: Seeing the women was wonderful. For nearly a month we hadn't known what happened to them. We had no idea they were in a compound with other women prisoners attached to that *madrassa* we were in.

The Red Cross delegates were also very welcome, but they too were under restrictions. Unfortunately they weren't as helpful as we would have liked. Their concern was 'Are you being looked after all right?' But that wasn't what we were bothered about. We wanted to know what was happening about getting us out.

❧

The whole situation was extremely tense. The Taliban's attitude to Westerners was aggressive and hostile. Although the ICRC delegation promised to return regularly to bring medical supplies and pass on post, they were never allowed back again.

But there was another surprise in store. The next day the diplomats, along with Heather's father and Dayna's mother, were finally allowed to visit the prison, although only for a very short period. Under the watchful eyes of their guards, the prisoners were led one after another into a meeting room with the diplomats from their country: first the Germans, then the Australians and finally the Americans. Going last meant that Heather and Dayna were at least able to speak with their parents a few minutes longer than might otherwise have been possible.

The Germans were allowed just five minutes with their diplomats, Helmut Landes from Islamabad and

Erna Salimi, an employee of the German embassy in Kabul who was still living in the city. Then the Australians saw the consul from the Australian High Commission in Islamabad, Alastar Adams. Last of all, the Americans spoke with David Donahue, the US consul general to Pakistan.

The prisoners were only allowed to say very general things. As soon as they mentioned something more personal, Najibullah Khan, a representative of the Afghan Foreign Ministry, would intervene to halt their conversations.

∽

DIANA: The Taliban were there throughout the meeting, interrupting us with their translations, listening to everything we were saying. That made me angry.

When the Australian consul asked Peter and me if there was anything we wanted to tell him, I snapped, 'No, I don't want to say anything in front of these people.' The injustice of our treatment got to me.

∽

KATI: Although the time we were allowed with our diplomats was disappointingly short, it did give us all renewed hope. We realised the world had not forgotten us. It was comforting to know that there were people out there working for our release. We felt confident there would soon be a solution.

We were also really pleased to receive the gifts our diplomats brought: several bags full of soap, creams, shampoo, food, sweets and snacks. It was like Christmas!

In return, we gave Ms Salimi a list of things we badly needed, in particular fresh clothes. We hadn't been allowed to return to our homes again to fetch any more things. Later we realised this was probably because by that point they had already been plundered.

I felt extremely ashamed about our sudden 'wealth' as we returned to the other Afghan women. The worst thing was, we weren't allowed to share any of it with them. But we did manage to pass on a few things secretly by simply leaving them lying around or dropping them as we passed. Even then, many of the women were too scared to pick them up.

❧

PETER: I finally got a packet of good razor blades. To the annoyance of the Taliban, I didn't have a beard. Being clean shaven was my form of protest. But I had run out of blades, and my appearance had started to look a bit wild.

All the snacks they bought, which you wouldn't normally think twice about, were suddenly a real treat. But the best thing for me was the fresh injection of hope that things would now finally start to move.

❧

MARGRIT: During the three weeks of our imprisonment, my thoughts had often turned to my parents. They were already elderly, and I worried about whether the news of my imprisonment might prove too much for them. I somehow cherished an irrational hope that they may not have heard about our arrest. The communication out of Afghanistan tends to be generally quite difficult, so I hoped that they might not think it strange that I hadn't been in contact for three weeks.

When I asked Ms Salimi whether it was possible that the newspapers in Germany had not reported our arrest and that my parents might not be aware of my predicament, she looked at me dumbfounded. 'Don't you realise the whole world is talking about you at the moment?' she asked.

She told me about the huge media interest surrounding our case. I quickly abandoned any hope that my parents could still be blissfully ignorant. I felt badly for them and wished I could tell them there was no need to worry about me.

SILKE: I was deeply disappointed by the meeting with the diplomats and Dayna and Heather's parents. We had waited for so many weeks and were then only allowed such a brief time with them. We were continually interrupted and weren't even allowed to say how we were really doing.

I was so furious that I needed to discharge some of my anger. As an artist, I find the best way to do that is through drawing. So I began to paint a huge mural—about two metres long—on the rear wall of our cell. Our overseer showed no opposition to the plan, but then she didn't realise my intention.

I mixed my colours using dirt, Nivea cream, Vaseline and washing-up liquid. With a nail file, I sketched the outline of a landscape with lots of animals and began to pour out my frustration into my work, while the others fired me on.

I felt particularly sorry for Heather and Dayna. Their parents had waited for weeks to see them, and then they had only been allowed five minutes together. When I then heard that they would only be able to see their parents every five days, and only for half an hour, my fuse blew.

For every day they weren't allowed to see their parents, I decided to paint a pig on the wall in revenge. The others stopped me. Pigs are considered unclean in Islam, and they didn't wish to cause offence. I grudgingly acquiesced.

∾

After the diplomats' visit, conditions for the foreigners in the prison began to improve slightly. Occasionally Georg and Peter were even allowed to sit outside for a short time in the late afternoon or evening, or to take a brief walk in the prison courtyard.

Another reason for this improvement was that Georg continually sought to befriend his guards. Again and again he would approach the Taliban and engage them in conversation, invite them into his cell and ask about their families. He had known and worked in their culture for many years and knew their customs.

Some of the younger Taliban were very dismissive of these gestures and remained cold and hostile. But with other guards Georg would sometimes sit chatting for hours. Genuine friendships began to build. Some guards even went so far as to pass on political information and let him know about the forthcoming arrival of the diplomats. They also smuggled short notes back and forth to the women.

Georg even tried to befriend the prison director, a task which cost him a great deal of effort. This was the man who destroyed the prisoners' letters to their families. He regularly beat up some of the Afghan prisoners and had been extremely aggressive during Georg's interrogation. But with time, Georg's politeness paid off.

Diana's fifty-first birthday was on 30 August, and as the day approached, Georg dared to ask whether the eight prisoners could get together and celebrate.

'For us foreigners, birthdays are an extremely important occasion,' he explained in effusive language. 'It's a big day, and Diana would be very, very sad if we weren't able to congratulate her on this important occasion.'

As a rule, Afghans don't celebrate their birthdays at all. Many don't even know their exact date of birth. But amazingly, the Westerners were allowed to meet together for breakfast on Diana's birthday. The women were brought into the room where the men had previously been interrogated. During their little party, they left the door as wide open as possible so that everyone would be able to see that nothing untoward was going on in this mixed gathering. Together they sang 'Happy Birthday' to Diana.

Diana had wished for nothing more for her birthday than to celebrate with the others. So the unexpected permission to breakfast together was a wonderful present. Georg pulled out the carefully treasured chocolate bar received from Marianne on his first day in prison and gave it to Diana.

After this unexpected concession from the prison director, Georg decided to risk asking whether they could meet again for an evening meal. He initially received no reply. But Georg's friendly guards must have petitioned passionately on his behalf because just before evening fell, they suddenly received permission.

The women were not expecting to meet up with Georg and Peter again. Margrit had ordered special food from the market as a birthday surprise for Diana: *degi kebab* and Afghanistan's national dish, *kabuli palau*, consisting of pieces of fried mutton together with rice, raisins, carrots and beef.

The women were just arranging for two portions to be sent over to the men's prison when a guard arrived to pass on the news that they could eat the meal together.

All agreed that the time spent together was a far greater treat than the food itself. They were only allowed a little more than half an hour, but in that time they were able to chat, swap news and pray for blessing on Diana for the coming year.

⤸

DIANA: Not everyone is able to celebrate a birthday in prison. I will never forget that day. I had prayed, 'God, all I want for my birthday is to be able to have a meal with Georg and Peter', and God gave me that request—not once but twice.

Silke drew a beautiful coloured card with a flying

kangaroo holding a birthday cake, and everyone wrote some choice words on it. That meant a great deal to me.

The Afghan women also knew it was my birthday because that morning Alastar Adams, the Australian consul, brought me some flowers picked from the UN compound, where he was staying. When we returned from our evening meal in the men's wing, the women also had a surprise ready: they threw confetti over me and then proceeded to perform various dances.

Fortunately our overseer wasn't there that evening, so the women felt more at ease. The washing bowls were again brought out for drums and each woman danced for me in her individual and very graceful manner. Then they showed us what to do and we had to join in!

I kept thinking: *This is unforgettable. No dictator will be able to break the spirit of these wonderful people. This is their heritage: laughing, singing and dancing. Even in prison, these brave women won't allow themselves to be broken.*

SILKE: In a later delivery from the German Embassy in Islamabad, we received a beauty box full of cosmetics, powders and creams. These afforded us many hours of amusement. But they also meant we could look after our appearance each day—after all, we had no shortage of time. These beauty sessions were good for our self-discipline. We wanted to be careful not to just let ourselves go because of the situation we were in.

We even found nail polish in the box. We painted our fingers and toes, much to the delight of the Afghan women.

For them, such a frivolity could have cost them the amputation of their fingers. But we foreigners were not subject to this law.

I think for them it was as though we were protesting on their behalf.

5

Charged Under Sharia

At about ten o'clock on the morning of Saturday 8 September, Georg and Peter were sitting on their mattresses chatting as was their habit around that time of day. Suddenly a Taliban guard stormed into their cell and hustled them outside.

'Get out, now! Move! You're being taken away.'

'What do you mean? Where are we going?' demanded Peter.

'Hurry up!' barked the guard in reply.

This was the nerve-racking practice of the Taliban. They were always hectic in their dealings with the prisoners, creating stress and feeding uncertainty. Georg didn't even have time to comb his hair, let alone change his crumpled *shalwar kamiz*. He was just able to pull on a vest jacket as he went out the door.

As they entered the courtyard, they saw a group of Taliban milling around a van. A short while later, the women were also led into the yard. They looked at each other in surprise. What were the Taliban planning?

They were ushered into the vehicle and immediately set off. The prison director led the way in a jeep, with at least six armed Taliban following behind in an open pick-up. The heavily guarded convoy made its way slowly through the city.

'Where are they taking us, Georg?' asked the others.

'I have no idea,' he said, straining to see out of the window and get his bearings.

Inside the van, the aid workers went through a mixture of feelings, from curiosity and uncertainty to near-panic. This was tempered to some extent by the joy of seeing a little of their surroundings and the fact that they were all together for the first time in over a week. They quickly exchanged news and talked about how they were getting on.

It was wonderful after a month to leave the close confines of the prison and to be able to observe every-day life in the streets of Kabul. Soon they recognised where they were—the van was driving towards Wazir Akbar Khan, the district where nearly all the aid workers lived. Georg was even able to look down his street as they drove past and spot his house in the distance. When they reached the big roundabout on Kabul's main road, their convoy suddenly turned off in the direction of the airport.

Are they taking us to the airport and just letting us leave the country? wondered Georg hopefully.

Little did he know that Afghanistan's Supreme Court was also on that road, just to the right of them. The convoy slowed down and pulled up at the road-side. The aid workers could hardly believe what they saw: an army of reporters and camera teams jostling to get near the van. Flashlights flickered incessantly, accompanied by a steady clicking of cameras. For a while they didn't know what was happening.

Somewhat overawed by the scene, the group climbed out of the van nervously. They were immediately led up the front steps into the antechamber leading to the courtroom. By this time everyone had realised they were at the Supreme Court where normally only the most important cases and heinous crimes were dealt with.

∽

MARGRIT: The Taliban who had conducted our interrogations had never mentioned any word of a trial. They'd always led us to believe we'd be released soon or at worst deported. Only Dayna's mother had hinted on a visit that we could face a trial.

When the guards loaded us into the van that morning, we had no idea where we were going. The sight of the court building was quite a shock for us, as was the throng of paparazzi.

∽

DIANA: When we saw all the photographers and media people waiting for us, I whispered to the girls, 'Quickly, cover your faces.' We all pulled down our *chadors*. The prison warden with us was wearing a *burka*.

As I got out of the van holding Heather's hand, a reporter shouted a question at us. We pushed past him.

'Just leave us alone,' I said. 'Leave us alone.'

❧

The aid workers had to wait for about twenty or thirty minutes before they were allowed into the courtroom. During this time, a female overseer was with them to 'guard over the honour of the women'. As she did not speak English, the team were able to talk without being interrupted.

This was the first time they had really been able to discuss the accusations made against each one during their interrogations. It was also an opportunity to uncover some of the lies they had been told about the confessions the others had supposedly made.

Georg, for example, had been told that Heather and Dayna had admitted to converting the Afghan family they visited to Christianity. They immediately put the record straight.

The women, on the other hand, had been told that Georg had fired Kati in disgust over her alleged behaviour and replaced her with someone else. The Taliban had said that Georg had admitted to all kinds of things, such as hiding piles of Bibles, Christian CDs and videos in Afghanistan's two main languages in their houses. Georg was even supposed to have apologised for proselytising among the Afghans.

They were all now able to reassure themselves that these had simply been lies, designed to play one off against the other and thus extract false confessions from them.

'Yes, we did show the Afghan family the documentary about Jesus,' Dayna said. 'But I had a funny feeling about it right from the start. The Afghan women were so insistent that we show it. I also realise now why the little boy had demanded—almost brazenly—that I give him my book.' Several days previously, the boy had come to Dayna's gate with some friends asking for a children's storybook containing Christian stories. He left when Dayna refused to give it to him, but not before displaying his anger with surprising vigour.

Heather explained that during their interrogations, she and Dayna had been keen to protect the Afghan family. 'We told the Taliban it had been our idea to visit the family and give them a copy of the book. I presume the family was forced to invite us. We admitted talking with them about religious things as people do everywhere here. But that was all.'

Kati had also been questioned about the film. But during her interrogation, the Taliban had focused more on her children's project, accusing her of operating it illegally. But she too had stuck to her guns.

The other four—Peter, Diana, Margrit and Silke—clearly could not be linked with any potentially dubious practices. But the Taliban had done their best. They accused them of being involved in the children's project and of possessing forbidden literature and radio cards. As none of this was true, they had refused to sign any confession.

The court really didn't have very much on any of them. They began to feel intrigued as to how things would proceed.

Finally they were led into the courtroom. It was not as big as they had expected, but it was packed with people. The defendants were taken to a row of seats at the front. Behind them sat Heather and Dayna's parents and the diplomats, who had found out about the trial at the last minute, virtually by chance. They in turn had informed the international media. As a result, the rest of the room was filled with countless reporters who were allowed to be present but not to take photos.

Georg was relieved to see the German diplomat from Pakistan, Helmut Landes, sitting behind him. They waved to each other briefly. Helmut Landes had spent the last two weeks in Kabul, fighting tirelessly for the release of the Shelter Now team. He intended to stay in Kabul for as long as it took. Georg and the others were particularly grateful for his efforts.

SILKE: I looked around at the room and all the people. At the front was a huge desk stacked with big heavy books. The wall behind was adorned with a large framed picture displaying verses from the Koran. Swords were fixed to the right and left of it along with a leather whip of the kind carried by the Vice and Virtue Police. The whip had a short handle to which a leather-encased steel cable was attached.

The Chief Justice, Mullah Noor Mohammed Saqib, sat at the desk in a large chair. He wore an enormous white turban and black tunic and had a cold, hard expression on his face. Around twenty other judges sat to the right and left of him, all wearing turbans and long beards. Most of them were quite old and wore very grave expressions which I found rather threatening.

To the left of the desk was a row of other men who sat on the floor, busily scribbling down everything that was said. It was like a scene from a medieval film. To the right of the desk stood the translator, who needed a good deal of assistance from the audience as he attempted to translate what the Chief Justice was saying into English.

∽

The language used in the courtroom was Pashtu, so Georg was able to understand a good percentage of the speech directly—a particular blessing as the translator proved to be of little help. In any case, the Chief Justice spoke at such great length before pausing for the translation that the English could at best be a sketchy summary of the original.

The Chief Justice's speech was essentially one long monologue extolling the virtues of *sharia*. He appeared to have made up his mind already about the verdict. He emphasised that the sentence handed down for the aid workers' 'crimes' would be in accordance with *sharia*, and could involve fines, imprisonment or even execution. The Taliban justices were currently in the process of studying the Islamic law with regard to the case, and they would, when finished, pronounce a just sentence on this basis. But the final word would be given to the supreme leader of all believers, Mullah Mohammed Omar. The defendants had the 'full right' to defend themselves and engage a lawyer of their choice.

'*Sharia* law is full of mercy and justice,' he concluded, a phrase which later became a standing joke among the group.

After the Chief Justice's speech, the defendants and their diplomats were allowed to speak. Georg took the opportunity to air his grievances to the court in the presence of the international press.

'We've been interrogated here for three weeks,' he said. 'No one has even told us what we are charged with and why we have been imprisoned. What crime are we supposed to have committed? Four of our staff can have absolutely nothing to do with this case and have clearly been imprisoned unjustly. Why have we not been allowed contact with the outside world? So far, we haven't even been allowed to talk to our families.'

Throughout this damning indictment of the Taliban's legal system, the Chief Justice did not condescend to even glance at Georg, let alone reply.

'You said we could have hired a lawyer of our choice,' Georg continued, 'but how could we do that when we weren't even aware that this court hearing was coming up and were forbidden to talk to our diplomats?'

Afterwards, Helmut Landes stood up on behalf of the diplomats and demanded better contact with the defendants so as to help them prepare their defence.

Silke also seized the opportunity to point out the injustice of her imprisonment. 'I have been held prisoner here in contravention of every human rights agreement.

Throughout my interrogation, I provided adequate proof that I have not been involved in any law-breaking activities. I had only been in the country a couple of days when I was arrested, having spent a number of months in Germany. I had no opportunity to commit a crime even if I'd wanted to. What crime am I accused of anyway? Why are my letters not being passed on? Why am I not allowed to speak to my family?'

Peter also jumped up, complaining that he had only been interrogated for a few hours, that the Taliban clearly had nothing on him and that he himself had no idea why he was in prison.

❦

PETER: I spoke pretty bluntly. I wasn't nervous that if I complained too vigorously it would go against us in some way. In that kind of situation you know you haven't got too much to lose.

After you've lived in a culture for a period of time you know in some measure what you can get away with. You can be very forceful with these people, but you have to know when to draw back or get a rifle butt in the ear. I hope I had some wisdom and tact, but I was never timid with these guys.

❦

Apparently unmoved, the Chief Justice adjourned the proceedings, saying the Supreme Court must investigate the charges further but that he would instruct the authorities in charge to facilitate the search for a lawyer. A new trial date would be arranged, he said, once a lawyer had been found and the court had completed its investigations.

The defendants were immediately whisked outside and deposited in the waiting van. It all happened so quickly that the assembled journalists were hardly able to get pictures, let alone ask questions.

⤚

GEORG: This first court appearance was the day before my father's birthday. It was very important to me to be able to send him a greeting and to let him know that I was well and he shouldn't worry about me. It pained me to think that my parents had no news about me. I wondered how they would be coping with my arrest. It must have been a terrible worry for them.

Our family is very large; I have seven brothers and sisters and we are quite close. So birthdays are always a big event in our family. Wherever I've been in the world, I've always called my father on his birthday. But this year I wasn't even able to write.

Looking at the myriad of paparazzi in front of our van, I knew I had to seize my chance. Quickly pulling open the side window, I lent out as far as I could and waved, calling, 'Please tell our parents not to worry. We are all well!' I then smiled confidently into the wall of cameras, my thoughts only with my father.

The guards were not at all happy about this little performance. But by the time they realised what was going on, it was too late.

◈

After his release, Georg heard that this brief scene had gone around the world, providing comfort not only to his own parents but to all those who were thinking, praying and worrying about the Shelter Now team.

The day before, Georg's parents had read a press report which included a photo of the four German prisoners juxtaposed with a photo of three badly beaten men hanging on a gallows. The picture had deeply shocked them. Now they were sitting in their lounge room watching the news when suddenly they saw Georg smiling into the camera and heard his message for them. It was his father's best birthday present that year.

Kati's mother, who was also watching the news that evening, was similarly encouraged. 'If Georg still looks so healthy, then my daughter must be doing okay as well,' she reasoned.

Sharia—The Islamic Law

Sharia (literally 'path') is the Islamic law. The Koran is often considered to be the source of *sharia*. However, *sharia* actually dates back to the early Middle Ages, between 700 and 900 AD. It was Islamic legal scholars who, in the absence of sufficient details in the Koran for state legislation, decided to draw up a codex of general legal principles covering family law, criminal law, inheritance law and, most importantly, religious rites and duties.

Over the course of time, various legal schools have grown up within Islam, with the result that *sharia* now tends to be applied differently from one Islamic state to another. Some consider *sharia* simply as a guideline for each individual's personal life with Allah while others, like the Taliban, are fierce proponents of *sharia* as the basis for the state administration of justice.

Like all Islamic fundamentalists, the Taliban rejected any precise exegesis of the Koran, preferring instead to interpret their religious sources as they saw fit.

The way in which *sharia* was applied in Afghanistan under the spiritual head Mullah Omar far exceeded the practice of other Muslim states in its level and extent of cruelty.

The group was taken back to the prison, with the usual band of armed Taliban in tow. Feelings in the back of the van were mixed.

They were still stunned by the onslaught of reporters and cameramen. They had previously had no real conception of how much media attention their case had attracted. What was the press saying about them? Would it work in their favour? Perhaps the world community would push harder for their release as a result of what it saw today. Or had the whole thing simply been a trick by the Taliban to push their regime into the public eye and defame Christianity?

They were deeply perturbed that the Supreme Court had been brought in to deal with the case and that they were to be tried under Islamic law. The possibility of the death penalty was a real shock. They had never reckoned on such harsh treatment.

The Chief Justice was not unknown to Georg. Noor Mohammed Saqib was a hardliner; as a close associate of Mullah Omar, he was greatly feared in Afghanistan. He had passed countless death sentences and never went anywhere without an army of bodyguards for fear of revenge attacks. They could expect no mercy from him.

With the situation obviously more dangerous than ever, one thing was clear to all: they urgently needed a good lawyer, preferably one who was familiar with *sharia* law. The whole procedure was obviously going to take a long time. All hopes of a quick release were abandoned.

Two days later, on Monday 10 September, the foreign diplomats were permitted to visit the aid workers to advise them on choosing a lawyer. A judge and a representative of the Afghan Foreign Ministry were also present. The diplomats suggested a Pakistani lawyer, Atif Ali Khan, from Peshawar. He was fairly young, but he had studied *sharia* law and would no doubt be able to represent them well. All eight prisoners agreed.

But it was to be another two weeks before they were finally able to meet him. The events of the next day, 11 September, not only shook the United States and the whole Western world, but also dramatically increased the danger faced by the eight Western prisoners in Kabul.

☙

Georg: I was sitting in my cell reading when suddenly the door was ripped open and two of the Taliban guards I had befriended charged into the room. They were clearly very agitated.

'Mr George, we've just heard on the radio that two aeroplanes have crashed into the World Trade Center in New York. The twin towers have collapsed and thousands are thought to have been killed. The Americans are saying it was a terrorist attack and Osama bin Laden was behind it.'

They were clearly very anxious. In fact, they were taking a huge risk in even telling me about it. I had won a number of friends among the guards over the previous weeks. They kept me up to date with the news and also smuggled letters back and forth between ourselves and the women. But they faced increasing risks. Their more hardline colleagues had grown suspicious and now kept close tabs on them. We later discovered that many of the guards were overjoyed that the Americans, whom they despised, had in their eyes finally got what they deserved. They cheered their hero Osama bin Laden.

A horror film began to play itself out in my mind. I knew immediately what this terrorist attack could mean for us prisoners and what would happen next.

Osama bin Laden was a close friend of Mullah Omar, and was of course living in Afghanistan, where his fighters also received training. Many of them fought alongside the Taliban. It was clear to me that the United States would demand the extradition of bin Laden, Mullah Omar would refuse and the Americans would respond with a military attack on the country. That would probably develop into a full-blown war, all the foreigners (including our diplomats) would leave Afghanistan, and we would be left behind as the only foreigners in the country. And we would certainly be used as human shields.

One thing was certain already. We would be totally at the mercy of the Taliban, who could use us to vent their anger against the West at any time without anyone being able to stop them.

This thought shook me to the core. During the previous seventeen years working in Pakistan and Afghanistan I had, on several occasions, experienced the wild fury of extreme Muslims and their resulting aggression against foreigners. Past scenes crowded into my mind of fanatical mobs charging through the streets, plundering shops and houses and threatening their inhabitants.

I was quite sure that the world would no longer be the same after 11 September. And we were going to be right at the centre of the storm.

Islamic Attacks and Their Repercussions for Shelter Now

After the 1988 bombing of Pan Am Flight 103 over Lockerbie in Scotland, American forces responded with a number of military assaults on Libya. All over Pakistan,

violent demonstrations were held against the Americans
and other Westerners as a result. It was simply too
dangerous for any foreigners to remain in Peshawar, and
the Shelter Now team was forced to flee to a safe place in
the mountains.

The 1991 Gulf War also proved critical for foreigners
in Pakistan. Georg knew immediately that the allied air
raids on Iraq would trigger a wave of anti-Western
demonstrations and attacks. A few hours before the air
raids began on Baghdad, he and his team fled to the
capital, Islamabad, for safety. The attacks had barely begun
when a mob of Islamic fundamentalists stormed into his
house in Peshawar. The Shelter Now team had escaped
literally at the last minute.

After the 1998 bombings of the American embassies in
Kenya and Tanzania, also attributed to al-Qaeda, all staff
were once again evacuated from Peshawar. For days they
lived with friends in Islamabad, in constant fear of being
discovered by extremists.

On Thursday 13 September, most Westerners left
Afghanistan: all United Nations staff, the employees of
other foreign aid organisations, and foreign business
staff and experts. The diplomats supporting the eight
prisoners were also forced to leave for their own safety,
along with Heather's father and Dayna's mother. Over
the next few days, the remaining Westerners followed.

Georg and Peter were very familiar with the sound
of the little planes operated by PACTEC (a humani-

tarian aviation agency) and the ICRC. They had often flown in them themselves. Now they heard them flying in and out of Kabul throughout the day, carrying all the Westerners out of the country.

Everyone has left us, Georg thought dejectedly. *Only God can stand with us now.*

A deep sense of apprehension spread among the Taliban guards. All were convinced it would be only a matter of time before the Americans took their revenge for the 11 September attacks. The guards whom Georg had befriended told him the Americans were in the process of building a global coalition against terror. And there was no doubt that the whole of the world's attention was now focused on Afghanistan. Georg learned that even Pakistan had sided with the United States, and the first aircraft carriers had already been dispatched to the region.

Anti-Western sentiment was now becoming increasingly evident among some of the guards. Georg and Peter were treated more strictly, and often threatened as though they were personally responsible for the trouble.

The whole situation is a tinderbox, thought Georg darkly. *I hope no one does anything rash.*

✧

PETER: When I first heard about 11 September, I thought the guards were lying. But then someone else who had been helping us said he had seen it on television, so I knew it was the truth.

Georg and I realised very quickly what it would mean. There had been rocket attacks for some smaller incursions before, but we knew that this time the Americans weren't going to stop at a couple of rockets.

Naturally I was concerned that this would mean an increase in hatred against foreigners, but mostly I was encouraged. I guess I sensed that 11 September was the last straw for the Taliban. I felt in a spiritual sense that God's judgment was on the government. Not on the Afghan people but on the Taliban regime. I didn't know how that was going to work out; I just hoped it wouldn't be in a grass-roots uprising that would kill thousands of the poor. But with 11 September, all of a sudden I felt that the end for the Taliban was going to be swift.

∽

In spite of the tense circumstances, the Pakistani lawyer, Atif Ali Khan, somehow found a way to get to his clients, although it took considerable patience on his part to circumvent all the hurdles placed in his way. When he finally arrived, on 17 September, he was accompanied by a colleague named Bismillah, who was not only a Pashtun but came from the same tribal region as the prison director. He had even studied at a *madrassa* where Noor Mohammed Saqib had taught for a while. This turn of events went a long way to placate the Taliban at the prison, who were not at all pleased that the prisoners had hired not just a lawyer, but a lawyer who claimed to be an expert in *sharia*.

First of all, Atif listened to his clients' story. He

was an extremely devout Muslim and right from the start very prejudiced against them. Prior to their first meeting, he had heard only negative information about them: they had reportedly distributed piles of Christian literature and Bibles and used their aid projects to bribe people to become Christians. What else could he think?

Shortly after Atif arrived, Georg took him to one side and asked him what kind of sentence he and his team might expect. 'Bearing in mind everything I've heard about you so far, I would say at least a prison sentence if not the death penalty,' the lawyer replied coolly. But he also emphasised that *sharia* was familiar with the principle of grace, and he would try to plead for this in their case.

The news shocked Georg deeply. He thought it best not to share it with the others.

The more the lawyer talked with his clients and dug around for evidence, however, the more amazed and indignant he became at how unjustly they had been treated by the Taliban. Nonetheless, he continued to believe in the concept of a fair trial and felt confident his clients would be released.

The lawyer also brought them clothes, newspapers and food from the diplomats and the Shelter Now team in Pakistan. He arrived laden with packages containing jumpers, warm underwear, socks, blankets, cosmetics, chocolate and snacks. It was all a very welcome surprise and helped lighten the mood among the eight inmates.

Best of all he brought letters. The Australian and American prisoners had previously received a little mail, but for the four Germans it was the first time they had received anything in the six weeks of their detention. Up until that point, nothing had found its way past the prison director because the Taliban had no way of translating the German to check what it said.

✎

GEORG: When Peter and I got back to our cell, I immediately opened my letters, my hands shaking as I did so. Seeing my children's handwriting and reading Marianne's letter assuring me they were all doing well moved me deeply.

At the same time it brought all the pain of separation flooding back with fresh acuteness. It was good to have Peter with me. He put his arm round me, comforted me and prayed for me. He could well understand my feelings; he had a daughter and a son of his own whom he missed deeply.

Among the things the lawyer brought was a fat envelope containing a collection of international press articles from the previous week. These focused in particular on our arrest and imprisonment. As I studied them, I began to appreciate for the first time the international dimension of our detention and the level of interest that our plight had attracted worldwide. The realisation came as quite a shock.

But I was deeply disappointed to read some articles. These were from newspapers which from the moment we were arrested portrayed us as a small band of fanatical Christians who had been evangelising at will in Afghanistan without any regard for the risks involved, either to ourselves or to the Afghans. We were not only given the blame for our own misery but also accused of jeopardising other aid organisations.

Why did some reporters suddenly believe all the lies and exaggerations of the Taliban without reserve? I couldn't understand it. The alleged evidence in the press photo they had released—a crucifix, an audio cassette, Bibles and other items—had never come from us. And in any case, it was laughable that someone should be sentenced to death for possessing such things.

The journalists knew the Taliban's total disregard for human rights and for anyone of another faith. They had robbed Afghan women of their rights, destroyed the historic statues of Buddha and were not in the least interested in the protests of the international community. They wanted to drive the Hindus out of their land and had forced them to wear pieces of fabric so they would be more readily identifiable—a macabre reminder of Nazi Germany where Jews were forced to wear the Star of David. In any case, we weren't the only ones to suffer harassment from the Taliban. Many other aid organisations had already undergone difficulties and had projects closed for minor 'offences'.

Why, I asked myself, did so few reporters make the effort to point out the success of our eighteen years of development aid in both Pakistan and Afghanistan? Why did so few write of all the dangers we had faced in trying to help the refugees, and the extent to which we and our work were recognised and appreciated in these countries? After all, high-ranking members of the Taliban had specifically asked us to work in certain regions of Afghanistan. They even gave us buildings and plots of land for our work, without charge. Many well-known aid organisations, various UN institutions and a number of Western governments had supported our projects with generous contributions, thereby expressing recognition of our work.

Even if two of our staff had shown a film about Jesus at the request of an Afghan family, that in no way justified the destruction of our entire organisation and our arrest. We would like to have been treated a little more fairly and respectfully by certain representatives of the Western press.

It took me some time to get over these newspaper reports.

On 30 September, exactly three weeks after their first hearing at the Supreme Court, the eight aid workers once again found themselves back at the court. In typical fashion, their trial date came up without any prior warning. They were bundled off in a whirl of action and with no mention of where they were going.

GEORG: What I found so terrible on this occasion was that they made a great detour. When we first set off, I assumed we were being taken back to the court, but then we took a different route, so I abandoned the idea.

They drove along the main road, heading directly for the Ariana Chowk—a notorious square where many death sentences were carried out. During every public execution the area teemed with spectators.

Surely they're not going to . . . ? I thought, with a sudden stab of pain in my chest.

I didn't tell the others of my gruesome fears. I ducked my head and peered out the front window, tension building inside me. *If there's a crowd when we get there, then I'll know what's going to happen.*

The square came into view. There was no crowd in sight. My relief was considerable.

It was awful the way the Taliban toyed with our emotions.

∽

This time when the group arrived at the Supreme Court, there was no throng of journalists waiting for them outside. Just one reporter from the Arab satellite channel al-Jazeera filmed the scene using a small video camera.

The proceedings were extremely disappointing for the aid workers. Owing to the imminent threat of a US bombing campaign, the hostility of the Taliban towards them was alarmingly tangible.

First of all, the team had to formally confirm their choice of lawyer. They were eager to finally discover the charges they faced, but the address and the charges were read out in Dari. No translator was provided for the defendants, and even the lawyers

were unable to understand anything because they
only spoke Pashtu.

'We need a translator,' protested Georg on behalf of
the whole group. 'How can we respond to the charges
if we can't understand them?'

His objection was ignored. The judges appeared to
be going through the motions of a trial for the sake of
appearances, little more.

'We need an English copy of the indictment,' Atif
added.

Surprisingly, a translation did actually turn up four
days later. But it was confusingly imprecise: names
were swapped round, and when it came to the details
discussed in the main body of the text, the English
was so bad in places that it was almost impossible to
decipher what was actually meant.

The lawyer was given fifteen days to prepare his
statement of defence. The aid workers, who had never
expected a fair trial in the first place, were now more
convinced than ever that they were de facto hostages.
No matter how watertight a defence their lawyer
delivered, the Taliban would do with them exactly as
they pleased.

❧

MARGRIT: The whole process at the court was a joke.
For example, in order to formally confirm our choice of
lawyer, all our photos were stuck into a big book and each
of us was then told to provide a thumb print next to our
picture.

We were unable to follow the reading of the charges in Dari, and when we finally received the English translation four days later, we had the very clear impression that the Chief Justice had not really registered who four of us were—Peter, Diana, Silke and myself—and had even got us mixed up at times.

For the first time, we were able to discover the charges against us. We were indignant about the laughably trivial and in many cases fabricated accusations levelled against us. It was unbelievable to think that this was why we'd spent the last nine weeks in that miserable prison.

PETER: The trial was a laugh. Not only could they not get the translation right, but most of us were charged by inference only—merely because we were associated with people or projects in the same organisation, or because the Taliban *thought* we were associated with those projects (even though in reality we weren't). They had no leg to stand on, not even as far as our lawyers were concerned.

The whole thing was simply a prolonged attempt to try to make something out of nothing. It increasingly looked like no decisions were going to be made anyway. Even some of the judges, old guys straight out of the bush, obviously didn't understand what was going on. The main judge, Noor Mohammed Saqib, had previously led a procession to try to burn the American embassy, so we weren't going to get much unbiased opinion from him either.

Excerpt from the Indictment of
Afghanistan's Supreme Court,
dated 4 October 2001

Facts

That Heather Mercer and Dayna Curry were arrested outside the
home of an Afghan family, located in Shairpoor, where they had
shown a CD on the life of Jesus Christ (May peace and
blessings of Allah be on him)* and gifted Photostat copies of a
children's book containing the stories of Jesus Christ (May
peace and blessings of Allah be on him) as stated in the Bible.
The said copies were in the languages of Persian and English.

That this incident led to the closure of SNI and the arrest of
the six more foreign workers and sixteen local workers on the
charge of proselytising.

Individual Charges

GEORG:

1. That it was his responsibility to prevent his staff from illegal
   activities;
2. That it is clear from the things belonging to ——— [a former
   Shelter Now employee] found in the house of Georg that he
   was involved in proselytising; and
3. That no formal permission was granted for the Children
   Project hence it is clear that the aim from the said project
   was to proselytise among the children.

HEATHER:

1. That she visited an Afghan family;
2. That she showed them a CD in which Jesus Christ (May
   peace and blessings of Allah be on him) is depicted as the
   son of God;
3. That she gave them a Christian children's book.

---

* A Muslim always adds the blessing of Allah when mentioning a
prophet's name.

DAYNA:
1. That she gifted a radio to the Afghan family;
2. That she gave a radio card to the Afghan family;
3. That she gave Photostat copies of a children's book on the life of Jesus Christ (May peace and blessings of Allah be on him); and
4. That she had shown a CD on the life of Jesus Christ (May peace and blessings of Allah be on him).

KATRIN:
1. That she visited two houses in the Shairpoor area and showed CD;
2. That she left a Dari Bible in the Afghan house.

DIANA:
That a radio card was found in her personal office hence it is clear she was proselytising.

SILKE:
That she visited Afghan houses and that she is an official of SNI.

PETER AND MARGRIT:
That they are Shelter Now employees and on the ground they were involved with the Children Project.

Atif sat down with the prisoners and went through each point of the charges with them so they could all respond to the specific allegations made against them.

Most of the points were twisted or complete invention. To use the few personal items left behind by a former employee as evidence that Georg had been proselytising was ridiculous. It was also not correct that the children's project had been opened without permission. Diana felt it a cheek that she should be accused of possessing a radio card, when she had

Excerpts from Official English Version of Decree

All foreigners in the Islamic Emirate of Afghanistan should take note of the following points:

1. They should not smuggle drugs.
2. They should not meet with or interview Afghan women.
   [. . .]
7. They should not copy or distribute magazines, books, newspapers or cassettes that are against the policies of the IEA.
8. They should not invite Afghans to other religions. [. . .]
11. They must respect the religion, faith and culture of the Afghans and should not work against the IEA.

In case of contravention of the articles 7, 8 [and] 11 the foreigner may be subject to 3–10 days in prison and then thrown out of the country within 48 hours.

Signed by Servant of Islam
Mohammed Omar
[Original decree was undated, but its official receipt in Kabul was dated 30 June 2001]

stated and written expressly during her interrogation that this was most definitely not the case. Peter and Margrit had not in any way been involved with the children's project. For the two of them and Silke, it was clearly a sufficient crime in the eyes of the Taliban simply to be employees of the organisation.

Atif promised to complete his letter of defence quickly and deliver it to the court. In view of the pitiful charges, he was optimistic the prisoners would soon be released.

The German embassy in Islamabad had also sent the lawyer a copy of the decree issued by Mullah Omar concerning proselytising by foreigners. This stated that foreigners who attempted to convert any Muslim to Christianity should be imprisoned for up to ten days and then deported, should the charges prove to be true.

The Shelter Now aid workers had already spent more than two months in prison without any satisfactory proof being put forward that they had tried to convert Muslims. But when the lawyer showed Mullah Omar's clear ruling to the justices at the court, they showed little interest.

Atif found in general that all manner of obstacles were placed in his way, preventing him from doing his job. The prison director suddenly decided to deny the lawyer access to his clients. When he went to the Supreme Court to complain, he was not permitted to speak to the justices. Various officials were suddenly not available or failed to process important documents.

Finally, on 5 October, an extremely irritated Mr Khan made an abrupt decision to drop everything and leave Kabul. Ostensibly he was returning to Peshawar to work on the case in peace, but more likely he was nervous about an impending US attack.

∾

On Sunday 7 October, US and British forces began their bombing campaign. Six days later, Atif returned and presented the aid workers with his letter of defence, including a statement that even under *sharia* law the eight had done nothing wrong and there was no justification to imprison them or put them on trial. Together they improved and changed a number of points. With this task complete, he drove to the Supreme Court to submit the documents.

The next day he visited the court again but returned frustrated. The Chief Justice had indicated it would take some time to review the case. Despite the prisoners' pleas, Atif decided to return to Pakistan to wait.

A week later he returned and drove yet again to the court. But this time he was not admitted to talk to anyone of any importance. The Chief Justice simply sent him a message that the court now had more important things to do than see to the eight defendants' case. Deeply depressed, Atif drove back to his clients at the prison. His painstakingly polished defence had not even been acknowledged.

Georg was not surprised. He had told Atif right from the start, 'This is not about having a fair trial. Whatever you submit to the judges, they will do with us as they please. We are hostages. There is no point in waiting for the end of the court proceedings. It's a waste of time. We have to think of something else.'

At the time the lawyer had not believed him, but now his experience was teaching him differently. 'Georg, I don't know what they're up to with you, but they're evidently not interested in justice,' he said dismally. 'We've reached a dead end. Only extreme pressure from your Western governments can help you now.'

The refusal of the court to deal properly with their case only confirmed what the aid workers had long suspected. They had realised almost immediately that they had been drawn into a trap by the Vice and Virtue Police. The real aim of the Taliban had been to destroy the aid agency and—as they were now beginning to realise—to hold its workers hostage for use as a bargaining tool with the West. The more they thought about this hypothesis, the more the pieces of the puzzle began to fit together.

In retrospect, they realised that the Afghan women had been unusually persistent in their requests for the Western women to visit them and had absolutely insisted that they wanted to see the film. The boy who had asked Dayna for a book had been uncharacteristically demanding. Then when Heather had left the Afghan family after her visit that Friday, she was not accompanied to the gate as usual by the women and a throng of noisy children. It was evident the family had known of the planned arrest.

The fact that the members of the Afghan family who had been arrested were apparently not held for long also gave rise to the suspicion that they had probably been pressured by the Vice and Virtue Police into inviting the aid workers over and persuading them to show a film they knew was forbidden. Dayna and Heather's being apprehended right in front of the house underscored this suspicion.

Finally, during the initial interrogation, the Taliban had continually spoken of three women who had visited the Afghan family. Although three had originally been invited, only two were in fact present that day. The interrogating officers thus appeared to have prior knowledge and had not immediately realised that the actual events had passed off slightly differently than planned.

The questions kept multiplying. Why had most of Shelter Now's aid projects been destroyed one day after their arrest and their houses plundered a short while later? Surely it would have been more reasonable to at least wait until the completion of the court proceedings, when the verdict would be clear. And if the Taliban were really interested in justice, as they claimed, why did they not simply observe the clear decree that had recently been passed down by Mullah Omar himself and deport the foreigners after ten days?

All this indicated that the Taliban's real interest was in eliminating the aid agency, and the trial was merely for the sake of appearances.

It also appeared likely that Mullah Omar—a close associate of Osama bin Laden who no doubt knew in advance of the plans for 11 September—had, right from the beginning, been looking for Westerners whom he could use as hostages to strengthen his position against the United States. When the aid workers were originally arrested, they were continually asked for the names of other Americans working with Shelter Now. The Vice and Virtue Police were apparently keen to get as many Americans in their custody as possible while appearing to have a legitimate reason for doing so.

In fact, on two separate occasions, Afghan Foreign Minister Wakil Ahmad Muttawakil did try to use the eight aid workers to bargain with the United States. The first instance was at the beginning of September, when he offered to exchange the prisoners for Sheikh Omar Abdel Rahman, who was serving a life sentence in the United States. The blind Muslim cleric was convicted in 1995 of planning a number of terrorist attacks, including the first attempt to blow up the World Trade Center in New York. Then, on 6 October, Muttawakil offered to release the eight in exchange for an assurance from US President George W. Bush that he would not proceed with military action against Afghanistan and instead begin negotiations.

The President refused, and twenty-four hours later the bombs began to fall.

Atif Ali Khan's failure at the Supreme Court showed beyond a shadow of a doubt that justice was not the issue for the Taliban. On the afternoon of 23 October, defeated and disappointed, the lawyer drove out of Kabul headed for Pakistan. He did not return again. The Taliban refused him any further access to his clients.

A few days later, the outside world lost all contact with the prisoners. No one knew how they were getting on or what was happening to them.

6

Hotel Hamid

On 17 September, the day the aid workers first met their lawyer Atif Ali Khan, a number of guards had marched into the courtyard of the women's section at the reform school prison.

'Pack your things now! We're leaving immediately! You're moving to another prison.'

None of the women had expected to be moved. Day after day, they had kept their hopes alive that soon they would be released. Now came this.

They tried asking the guards where they were going and why. The response was predictable: 'Quick! Get a move on!' There was little time to say goodbye to the Afghan women with whom they had lived, laughed and cried during the previous six weeks, and many of whom had become friends.

KATI: Without exaggerating, we hardly had time to bundle our few things together. The stress caused by the Taliban was obviously designed to intimidate us. They rushed in like a tide of panic and confusion.

The Afghan women were extremely dismayed to lose us

126

so suddenly. Mushtabah, the lady who had often come to our houses in the past selling embroidery, was appalled at the news and began to cry. I managed to say a secret, snatched goodbye to her in the bathroom. She threw herself into my arms sobbing and didn't want to let me go. We had become a support and source of hope to her in her captivity.

With a heavy heart, I pulled myself away. For days afterwards, I kept reliving that heartbreaking scene. Relief only came when I heard a short while later that Mushtabah had been released.

Over in the men's section, Georg and Peter got similar treatment. 'You're moving. The van's waiting. Jump to it!'

Georg tried to delay. 'What's going on? Who ordered this? We're not leaving. We're staying here.'

'No! That's an order.'

But the two men refused to move. In the end the prison director came in person.

'You have to go,' he confirmed. 'You don't have any choice. Anyway, we're taking you to a better place outside Kabul, safer and much nicer than here.'

Perhaps they'll put us under house arrest, the men thought hopefully. Both dreamed of exchanging their prison cell for a house again. They gathered their few possessions and trundled out to the van, where the women were already waiting.

Leaving the prison followed by the obligatory truckload of armed Taliban, the van drove off through the streets. The move had taken all eight prisoners unawares and some were quite distraught. But they took advantage of the rare opportunity to be together and swapped news. In the meantime, Georg kept an eye on the road to see where they were being taken.

After little more than ten minutes, the van drew up outside a large set of gates in the district of Sharinau. Georg knew these gates well. They were always guarded by Taliban, and he had often walked past them and wondered what might be inside. He was about to find out.

They drove through an archway. After about fifty metres they passed through another set of gates into a prison yard surrounded by high walls and barbed wire.

The aid workers protested immediately. 'You said you were taking us out of the city to a safer and better place. This is just another prison!'

'This is the new place,' they were told curtly. 'You're staying here. Get out!'

Again the prisoners had been deceived. The new prison was in the very centre of the city and, worse still, belonged to the intelligence service—an obvious target in any US bombing campaign. It was the women's second prison, the men's third.

Georg and Peter were barely able to say goodbye to their six colleagues before the women were whisked through a side door.

❧

SILKE: The new prison was a shock, especially after we'd been so gullible as to believe we were genuinely being transferred to a better place. The little courtyard of the women's section was a dry wasteland, surrounded by high walls and barren of any life. The clay ground was trampled down hard. On one side was a water pump, behind which stood a little wooden house with a hanging roof—was that perchance our toilet? I was disgusted.

We were hustled through the courtyard into the building where we were told to leave our things (such as they were). Everything was cramped, dingy and dirty.

I won't stick this out for five minutes, I thought, half panicking. The others felt the same, and we all stormed back out into the yard in protest.

Our new overseer returned and once again showed Diana and Heather the inside of the building. This second trip proved a little more promising as they discovered a proper toilet. But our new cell was just 4.5 metres square, and the window had been walled up.

'No way!' I protested. 'No one's getting me to sleep in that hole.'

The prison director—who immediately made a favourable impression on us—sent for some workmen. Within an hour the stones had been knocked out from the window frame and a pane of glass had been inserted. They even tried to clean the cell and put in proper beds. I had never seen anyone in Afghanistan work as fast as those men did.

In the meantime we sat out in the courtyard, shuffling from one corner to another to keep in the shade. In

September the Kabul sun still beats down with midsummer intensity.

Margrit was not feeling at all well. She was still struggling with the aftermath of amoebic dysentery and lay flat out on a mattress, exhausted.

After a while, we were brought plates of *kabuli palau*. It tasted far more delicious than anything we'd previously been served in prison. Slowly we began to believe that we had indeed been brought to a better place.

Three Afghan women, together with around nine children, initially shared that part of the prison with us. But they were moved after about three days. From then on, we had the area to ourselves.

We soon realised that our overseer, Mullah Hamid, was very well disposed towards us and allowed us a number of privileges. 'Hotel Hamid', as we called it, was to be our home for the next ten weeks.

⤜

On arriving at the prison, Peter and Georg were led into another courtyard belonging to the men's section. The men's prison itself was extremely old and dilapidated, with barred windows. Many of the inmates were standing around outside. Some showed signs of curiosity as the foreigners were brought in, but most just looked on apathetically.

Peter and Georg's first impression of the prison was terrible. Clutching their meagre belongings—a blanket and a plastic carrier bag each—they were led into the building through a huge and well-rusted iron door.

Inside it was so dark that at first they could hardly see at all. They stumbled up some concrete steps to the first floor. There they were led through another barred door and down a long dark corridor lined with prison cells. The door to each cell had been reinforced with steel, with only a small peephole left uncovered at about eye-level.

The doors were open and the inmates hung about in the corridor. They looked frightened and dejected, although they eyed the two foreigners with curiosity as they walked past. Some of the Afghans followed them down the corridor.

The cell given to Peter and Georg was just 2 metres wide by 3 metres long. The window was quite large and had bars across it. It looked out across a yard. Standing at the window, they could see the building was designed in an L-shape.

The cell itself was filthy, and the walls were covered with names and dates scribbled by previous prisoners. Steel shelves coated liberally with grime leaned against the left wall. A wobbly iron bed sporting an unbelievably grim mattress made up the rest of the furniture.

❧

GEORG: Peter and I sat down heavily on the bed and said nothing. We needed time to digest this latest turn of events. Again we had been lied to and tricked. Instead of a nice house, we had landed in the intelligence service prison.

A few Afghan inmates stood gaping at us silently from

the doorway. It wasn't difficult to read their thoughts: what were these two Westerners doing here? To their credit, they remained silent, clearly noticing how shocked we were.

After some time, one addressed me in Pashtu, asking if he could do anything to help. Their mouths dropped open again when I answered in fluent Pashtu. They were delighted. These sad and pitiful men suddenly came to life and began firing a barrage of questions at us.

After a while, I asked if anyone knew where we might find a second bed. Several men were on the case immediately. The others set to work with us, clearing and cleaning the cell as best we could.

It didn't take long for our fellow inmates to rustle up a second bed. Together we tried to manoeuvre it into our tiny cell. We finally made it, but that left us with an aisle of less than one metre between the two beds.

I could hardly bring myself to even touch the mattresses. The pillows had huge holes in them and were already well colonised by various bugs. Fortunately we still had a little money, so one of the guards went out and bought us some anti-vermin powder which proved effective. I laid my spare *shalwar kamiz* over the mattress by way of a sheet and covered the pillow with the spare towel I'd received from the diplomats.

With these few 'home improvements' complete, I decided to make a tour of our corridor in an attempt to acclimatise to my new surroundings. There were more culture shocks in store.

On reaching the toilets, I found that the wooden doors had rotted and fallen off their hinges. They had been replaced by a curtain riddled with holes. The toilet itself consisted of a platform with three holes, each full to the top with excrement. Throughout the time we were there, no one ever attended to that particular disaster. The stench was so foul I nearly vomited on the spot.

Continuing my tour, I discovered that around fifty inmates were held in this part of the building. They were permitted to walk up and down the corridor freely, with only the entrance barred and manned by guards. During the afternoons, prisoners were allowed outside into the court-yard for a while.

The opportunity to walk around was a huge relief after spending most of the last six weeks locked up in a cramped cell. Having free access to our co-prisoners was also a new experience.

࿇

PETER: The intelligence prison shocked me badly at first. The conditions were dreadful, and for the first time we were really locked up: this *was* a prison, with steel bars on the doors.

The thing that made the difference was the helpfulness of some of the prisoners and guards. Their willingness to find a second bed and help us clean the cell made us feel a bit better.

In one respect our situation had improved. In the first month we could only look out at daylight through the window—for much of that time we were not allowed out into the yard at all. But after a few days in the intelligence service prison, we were able to get out into the yard and into the sunshine regularly. Somebody had actually done a job on the yard: it was a nice grassed area with a plastic canopy shading various plants, almost like a little hothouse. It was marvellous to be able to get outside.

๑๖

GEORG: A new chapter in our prison routine began. Previously we had only had contact with our Taliban guards, but now I was able to talk to the other inmates. Through their stories I began to learn about an aspect of Afghan life which had been closed to me before.

Over the previous seventeen years I had met Afghans from all walks of life. I had chatted with wealthy Afghans in magnificent houses in Peshawar and Kabul. I had been a guest at extravagant weddings and dined with influential men in exclusive hotels. I had even won friends among high-ranking members of the Taliban.

At the other end of the scale, I had spent a lot of time with Afghan refugees in the camps we had built. I had listened to their stories of pain and suffering and their odysseys across Afghanistan. Many had fled from the Taliban. Others had been forced to leave their houses and fields because they were no longer able to feed their families after years of drought.

I had sat in remote Afghan villages eating with leaders of various tribes, including leaders of the Mujahedin. Some of them were real adventurers, keen to show off their huge arsenals of weapons. I had spent the night in *hujras*—Pashtun guesthouses—and drunk tea with nomads who moved with their tents across Afghanistan's steppe region. I was familiar with life in the city and life in the countryside. I was acquainted with the lives of both the rich and the poor.

But I had known nothing of the life of Afghans as revealed to me there in the intelligence prison. I had heard about it before, but I had never imagined that the suffering could be so indescribably great. Behind those prison walls, I realised that since the overthrow of the last king of Afghanistan in 1973, almost every family in the country had suffered untold disasters. People had lost their possessions, been driven from their homes, suffered arrest, torture, execution. Almost every Afghan family had lost loved ones during the previous twenty years or so.

Thus I discovered an area of Afghan life which shocked me to the core, and deepened my love for the Afghans all the more. I felt that all the deprivations of this hideous prison were worth it to gain such an authentic insight into the lives of everyday Afghan people.

Right from the first day I built up friendships with these men, each of whom had a unique and tragic tale to tell. They would crowd into our cell, sitting down on the beds or floor, and we would talk about our lives, sometimes until late into the night. I tried to help them where I could, encouraging them and handing out medicines. Since we now began to see the women more often, I borrowed some money from Silke, who had managed to smuggle a lot more into prison than the rest of us. This meant I was able to give some to the other inmates and their hungry relatives.

Afghanistan—A Broken Land

Afghanistan is one of the poorest countries on earth, not least because the land is so difficult to farm. In many areas, a modest level of agriculture can only be supported through intensive irrigation. The northeastern and some central parts of the country are dominated by virtually impassable mountains and high-lying valleys which are difficult to access.

The prolonged drought of recent years has led to a huge refugee movement within the country—the hard-baked earth no longer yields enough to feed its residents. Many families have been forced to leave for the impoverished refugee camps on the border with Iran or in Pakistan, in the hope that there they will receive enough food to survive. Worse than the drought has been the warfare which has raged for more than two decades, bringing untold suffering. By the time the Taliban arrived on the scene in 1994, the people were war-weary and without hope.

In 1973, King Zahir Shah was overthrown in a military coup led by his cousin, Prince Daoud Khan. Khan abolished the monarchy, declared himself president and established the Republic of Afghanistan. Although he tried to improve the living conditions of ordinary people and drew up a constitution enshrining some rights for women, his rule was essentially a dictatorship.

In April 1978, President Daoud was murdered in a communist coup. The new communist government nullified the constitution, banned all Islamic rites and traditions and launched an intensive modernisation

program. A resistance movement was born and the
country plunged into civil war.

In December 1979, Soviet military units marched into
the country, in the mistaken belief that they could quickly
quell the unrest. However, it was the era of the Cold War,
and Western powers were keen to ensure the Soviets did
not extend their sphere of influence. They armed and
financed voluntary resistance armies made up of Afghans
and Arabs, known as *Mujahedin* ('warriors for Islam'). The
ensuing Soviet war in Afghanistan lasted ten long years, at
the end of which the USSR admitted defeat and withdrew.

But even then, the ethnically divided country did not
find peace. Instead, a civil war raged on between the
Afghan communist government and the Mujahedin.
When the government was finally overthrown, the various
Mujahedin factions continued to fight among themselves
for control of the country. They ravaged a number of cities
in the process, most notably Kabul.

Around 1.5 million people are believed to have been
killed during the years of war. Many millions more were
forced to flee the country, or became displaced within
Afghanistan itself. It was the ordinary people who suffered
most from the fighting between the various warlords and
their followers. By 1994, radical Islamic Taliban had
emerged from among the Pashtuns, vowing to restore law
and order. They quickly defeated their opponents, taking
power across the country.

The mainly non-Pashtun factions of the Mujahedin
agreed to join forces against this new common enemy and
formed the Northern Alliance.

In September 1996, the Taliban took Kabul from the
Northern Alliance, going on to control around 80 to
90 per cent of the country. As the Taliban were essentially
made up of Pashtuns, they tended to oppress the people
of other ethnic groups such as the Tajiks, the Hazaras and
the Uzbeks. In the meantime, they continued to wage war
against Tajik commander Ahmed Shah Massoud, by far the
most powerful Northern Alliance leader, who had been
able to retain a stronghold in the north of the country.
   The Taliban were particularly cruel to followers, or
perceived followers, of Massoud. He was murdered, almost
certainly by members of al-Qaeda, just two days before
the 11 September attacks.

The regular 'meetings' of prisoners in Georg and
Peter's cell were sadly not tolerated for long. The prison
directors became suspicious and sent along spies to
find out what the discussions were about. Finally they
banned the Afghans from having such frequent contact
with the foreigners.

So Georg changed his tactics. Every now and then
he would wander along the corridor to various cells,
chatting a little here and a little there, and soon
befriended nearly all of the fifty inmates.

Very few of the Afghans at the prison were Pashtuns.
Many were followers of Ahmed Shah Massoud, the
recently murdered leader of the Northern Alliance.
They came, both young and old, from all over Afghanistan, and they had been imprisoned simply because

they belonged to the wrong group or had been accused of collaborating with opposition movements. One group of very respectable elderly men with white beards had clearly not seen eye to eye with the Taliban on some matter and ended up in prison as a result.

Then there were a number of simple nomads, known as Kuchi, who had evidently been minding their own business, content to roam across the region with their camels and goats, and with very little interest in, or knowledge of, politics. They had been locked up on charges of supporting the ex-king. Georg talked with them for a while and discovered they did not even know the name of the deposed monarch. Fortunately, their tribe was able to pay some hefty bribes, and soon afterwards they were released.

Another inmate had owned a stationery store in which henchmen of the Vice and Virtue Police had found postcards depicting Indian actresses. He was serving a six-month jail term.

But it was the followers of Massoud who were hunted down most energetically by the Taliban. Anyone even suspected of sympathising with Massoud was arrested and brought to the intelligence agency prison. An uncorroborated claim from a neighbour with a grudge was sometimes enough to get a man incarcerated. Most of these men spent between six months and a year at this prison before being sent off to other prisons to serve out the rest of their sentences.

There were no lawyers who could seek to prove the innocence of these men. All their families could do was go to the 'judge' and try to negotiate with him directly. This generally involved paying a bribe. But the amount demanded was so large that many had no hope of paying. Some families were left destitute by their attempts to scrape together the money. One inmate told Georg that his family was in the process of selling their house to pay for his release. From then on, the whole family would have to live in a refugee camp.

Many prisoners were the only breadwinners for their families and extended families. These extended families often included sisters or sisters-in-law, with their children, whose husbands had been killed in war. They too were dependent on the one male relative for food. In the year 2000, more than 10,000 widows were listed in Kabul alone. So it is hardly surprising that many families were forced to sell all their possessions simply to survive. Those who had nothing left to sell went hungry.

The men who poured out their stories to Georg all told, without exception, of how they had been severely beaten after their arrest. They spoke of 'cables'—steel cables the size of a man's middle finger which were wrapped in plastic and used as whips.

'I got one hundred cables when I was arrested,' said one man.

'I got fifty cables a day,' said another.

Others described their torture in terms of time: 'I got two hours of cables.'

During their time in the intelligence service prison,

Georg and Peter often heard screams from the torture chamber, accompanied by the lashing of whips. They tried covering their ears but could not block out the sound. While the barbaric suffering continued, the two men would sit frozen to the spot, unable to do anything but pray: 'Lord, have mercy on them . . .'

❧

PETER: The torture of prisoners by the Taliban made me angry and frustrated. We knew who the perpetrators were, and when we met these officials, which we did fairly frequently, trying to be nice to them and bless them, as our faith required, was pretty difficult.

We got the brunt too in the sense that we had to buy drugs and try to help those who'd been beaten, some of them very badly. We weren't beaten ourselves, but the Afghan workers from Shelter Now were. It's nice to be privileged in that respect, I guess, but it's also extremely hard to hear people being tortured and to know that some are suffering almost on your behalf.

We were really tested in our faith because the only thing we could do about the whole thing was to pray.

❧

GEORG: During our times outside in the prison courtyard, I once noticed a man lying on the grass several days in a row. He was clearly writhing in pain. I finally went over to him, assuming he was ill and suffering from fever or diarrhoea. But he told me he was being beaten every day. He showed me his wounds and complained of intense pain.

I gave him the highest dose of painkillers I could lay my hands on.

The story of another man, an engineer, haunted me even in my dreams. I had noticed him straight away because of his friendly and helpful manner, and he became a real friend during our time in prison together.

He had been arrested by the Taliban after being libelled by his neighbour. Prior to that he had already spent seven years at the notorious Pul-e-Tsharki prison. For three years of that time, he had been chained up in an underground dungeon. He was unable to cut his hair or fingernails, and his lavatory was right there where he lay. Throughout this time, his family had no idea where he was and finally presumed him dead.

He told me about his loneliness and despair during those years. No one had ever come to visit him. His fellow prisoners were all eventually released or executed, but he was forced to vegetate alone in chains.

When he was finally released, he was mentally deranged and wandered through the streets unable to find his house. For a while he slept at a local mosque. When at last he arrived home, his family were overcome with shock at his appearance and condition. He was then told that both his father and brother were dead. His young wife was so traumatised by his state that she fell ill, and a month later she too died.

Of the many tragic stories I heard, this was perhaps the worst. But the amazing thing was, this engineer, who had suffered so much, was an unusually humble and helpful man. In fact, I discovered that many of those who had suffered the most terrible things imaginable displayed evidence of outstanding character. I noticed their sympathetic and helpful attitude, and the way in which they found real pleasure in the most trivial things. They were very different from the Afghans I knew 'outside'.

Obviously the terrible sufferings of some had left them permanently deranged. Others had been driven to seek solace in drugs. But I came to love them all genuinely.

Surprisingly few tensions or disputes arose between the inmates. The men interacted quite differently from the way one would imagine they would, or the way portrayed in films. Occasionally arguments flared between the representatives of various tribal groups, but even these never turned violent.

Of course, tensions were sparked when it emerged that some of the inmates had accepted bribes from the prison directors to spy on our conversations and friendships. I was particularly hurt to learn that one prisoner, whom I had often supported and supplied with medication, had chosen to run us down in front of the prison directors.

A letter written by Georg to Greg Gilmore, the director of the Shelter Now project in Peshawar, helps to illustrate the nightmare experiences suffered by the inmates of both prisons. This letter, like all of those included in this book, had to be smuggled out of the prison—initially by the aid workers' lawyer, Atif Ali Khan, and later by Afghan prisoners when they were released. In agreeing to take the forbidden correspondence these men often risked their lives. Any officially permitted letters were censored and not allowed to contain negative information.

25 September 2001

Dear Greg,

Finally I get the opportunity to send out some letters. One prisoner leaves tomorrow and wants to take them to Peshawar. We are not allowed to send or receive mail.

We are being held in the intelligence agency prison. I'll have a lot of horror stories to tell you once we are free. It is amazing what the women have had to endure. In the last prison, women prisoners were beaten in front of their eyes every day and sometimes we witnessed terrible beatings of boys in the madrassa. It is like one huge nightmare. But please don't say anything to Marianne.

It was awful to hear about the attacks on the World Trade Center in New York and the Pentagon in Washington.

The diplomats have now gone from Afghanistan, along with all the other foreigners, and we are left with these people. We were then shifted under heavy guard to a terrible prison. Greg, if you were to see it from the outside, you'd have a shock! We were told they were bringing us to a nicer place that would be safer for us, but it was exactly the opposite. When we went past the steel gates, everything was dark and as filthy as you can imagine. The atmosphere was terrible, and when Peter and I saw our cell we were utterly speechless. It is just 2 metres by 3 metres. Three holes serve as toilets for up to fifty people; they stink and are filthy.

Then we heard the stories of the prisoners. It is very, very sad and shocking what people here have suffered—

for nothing. It's terrible. Fear gripped me as I listened to their stories. Will we have to go through similar things? Who would be able to protect us then?

The prisoners are very kind to us and often try to encourage us. But, Greg, sometimes I think I can't take it anymore. Also I think so much of Marianne, Daniel and Benjamin. This separation is very painful for me. I have no news of them. How are they doing? How are they coping? I think of you all, the team, the future of our projects which we built up with so much hard work. And how we are probably being kept as hostages. They don't tell us anything about what they plan to do with us.

The situation is very tense here. The uncertainty is often unbearable. At least I'm allowed to visit the women every day. They always ask me for news of what's happening, but I can't tell them much. Greg, please tell all our friends not to stop praying for us.

There would be much more to share but that is enough for now. God has allowed us to go through this suffering and often we've cried out to him to make it stop—but things just seem to get worse. Please pray for us that we all come out unharmed.

We are in the fire and it's hot, but we cling on to him and his word and praise him in the most trying of circumstances.

Your friend
Georg

For the women, daily life in the new prison was much quieter, particularly after the Afghan women and children in their section were moved elsewhere.

The improved menu of their first day continued— the prison director's personal chef had been roped in to cook for them. With no other inmates to consider, they now felt free to allow themselves more extras from the market, particularly fruit and vegetables, and were even equipped with a little hotplate. Sometimes in the evening they would cook something themselves and have two portions sent over to Georg and Peter.

Every morning the women met together at ten o'clock. They discussed how they were coping, read the Bible together, sang and prayed. They usually had a similar meeting again in the evening.

Otherwise they tended to spend a lot of the time reading the books given to them by Heather and Dayna's parents and the diplomats. Once they had finished all these, they decided to make some cards for playing games.

KATI: We started playing memory and card games after Diana's birthday in August. We'd been able to smuggle in a few card games from our apartments when we were allowed home that one time. When we'd played them so much that they were nearly falling to pieces, we started to invent our own games using homemade cards. About once a week, we would all sit down for an evening games session. It was therapeutic to stop being so serious for a while and just have a laugh together.

Towards the end of our time in prison, our patience started to wear thin and we'd sometimes get on each other's nerves. We found these games evenings lightened the atmosphere and brought us closer together again, so we started having them more often.

Excerpt from one of Kati's letters to her mother

30 September 2001

. . . We've developed a new hobby: song writing! We're turning all the Bible verses that have helped us here into songs. Silke, Dayna and I take turns to compose a tune and then the others are called on to exercise their grey cells and learn them all. We're even talking about recording a prison CD when we get out—the Kabul Six— proceeds, of course, to Afghanistan. Well, we keep joking about it anyway.

DIANA: We developed a number of standing jokes during our time in prison. Anyone else would probably find them hard to understand, but to us they were hilarious. Margrit came up with the saying 'Teatime is over'. The 'Tea' meant 'T' for Taliban, and somehow every time she said it, we could hardly stop laughing.

We also used to laugh a lot about how when we were finally free we would form a band and call ourselves the 'Kabul Six' and go round singing our self-composed prison songs.

One time Dayna's mother, hoping to offer us some comfort, wrote that we shouldn't worry because, once we were released, we'd no doubt be signed up with first-class psychiatrists. My immediate thought was: *I don't need a psychiatrist—I need a hairdresser!* So then it became one of our standard phrases: 'Okay, I'll go and see a psychiatrist, just as long as he can fix my hair too.'

∽

Simple daily tasks such as washing clothes at the water pump, cleaning vegetables in purified water or keeping the bathroom clean took longer than usual. The women spent days scrubbing away at the bath and tipped gallons of bleach down the toilet until they felt proud to possess the cleanest prison bathroom in the whole of Afghanistan.

Furthermore, Mullah Hamid proved to be an extremely obliging overseer. When he said they would be able to meet with Georg and Peter every day, they initially didn't believe him. But he proved to be as good as his word. Daily he arranged visits in spite of the personal risk to himself. He was extremely concerned that one of his superiors, Mullah Yusuf, should not learn of their clandestine meetings.

Every afternoon the men were allowed into the women's prison, where their colleagues were awaiting them with fresh tea and coffee. They would spend about half an hour talking, and Georg, through his many conversations with his fellow prisoners, would always have plenty to pass on. News of political events unfolding in Afghanistan and the world was particularly important to the women. This daily half hour was their only opportunity to discover anything about life outside the prison walls.

⁂

DIANA: Every day, early in the morning, we would start asking, 'Would you please let Georg and Peter come today?' We had to go on like this all day. If we didn't ask, the two men wouldn't be allowed to come.

'Look, Georg is like our father,' we would plead. 'He and Peter are the only men we have to protect us.'

Most days they were allowed to come. We looked forward to their visits so much. We made coffee and shared biscuits with them, if we had some. Sometimes we'd say, 'Guess what? We've written another song', and we'd sing it to them. Usually we would just sit and talk, and perhaps pray for each other. Georg became like a pastor to us all— he would write to us too, encouraging us, advising us.

⁂

One evening—it was 4 October, the day they received the official English translation of the charges against them—the six women heard an unusual commotion coming from the courtyard. They could hear the voices of Afghan guards and a woman's voice shouting angrily in English.

All six rushed outside in an attempt to mediate. The new arrival was clearly incensed. She had apparently been told she was going to a hotel and was understandably not happy at ending up in a prison instead.

Grateful to encounter anyone speaking English, she paused for a moment. 'Are you the Christians the Taliban arrested and threw into prison?'

She introduced herself as Yvonne Ridley, a British journalist who had tried to disguise herself as an Afghan woman, donning a *burka* and entering the country illegally to report on the looming war and interview local Afghans. Just before crossing the border back into Pakistan, she had been discovered by a Talib and arrested.

Her story became world news. For three days she shared the prison with the Shelter Now staff before being released and allowed to return home. Through Yvonne, the world received the first news of the aid workers. During a television chat show, she was asked what impression she'd gained from the six women.

'Although they're all very different, they have one thing in common: they are strong women,' she answered. 'They radiate such a warmth. And they're modest too. Some people have said what I did was courageous, but these women really know what courage is. Their strong faith in God evidently helped them get through it all.'

She also talked about one evening when she was sitting outside in the yard reflecting on her predicament. 'I heard the others singing one of their self-composed songs, but at the same time I could hear the call to prayer bellowing out from a nearby minaret. It was so strange to hear this beautiful singing from inside the cell contrasting with the screeching from the minaret.

'I am very grateful to those women because they helped me get through those days in the prison.'

DIANA: They brought Yvonne into our cell and abruptly left. She was absolutely furious because the Taliban had told her they were taking her to where there were other foreigners staying in a hotel with satellite TV.

She took one look at our cell and said, 'What a hell hole.'

'Oh, I think it's pretty good,' I said. 'We've cleaned it up.'

She broke down and cried then because she'd been by herself for so long, having to be brave.

SILKE: Yvonne was brought to us one evening in a very angry state. We quickly made friends and I really enjoyed the time with her. She told us about many of the political developments that had occurred while we'd been in prison, of which we were unaware. I liked her forthrightness and her understanding of people. Even though we had to wait a lot longer for our release, we were genuinely pleased for her that she was able to return home so soon.

KATI: Yvonne was a welcome change for all of us. We particularly appreciated her information about what was happening in the world. She was the first one to give us a detailed report on the 11 September attacks. She also told us some great anecdotes from her life as a journalist—about the British Royal Family, for example. It was a real laugh.

But she was very provocative in her dealings with the

Afghan guards. She would often shout at them and once she even spat on the ground in front of their feet. We grew quite concerned for her safety.

She explained that she wanted to be the worst prisoner the Taliban had ever had. I think she may just have succeeded!

∽⬩

After three months of living together in extremely close confines, the appalling sanitary conditions, severe emotional strain and ever-prevalent fear of death all took their toll. On occasions personal crises and tensions within the group were hard to deal with. The six women came from three different cultures, and each had her own ways and habits that she was used to in areas such as eating or keeping order. Age differences were also marked, ranging from twenty-four to fifty-one—not to mention, of course, personality differences and varying abilities to cope under pressure.

All this meant the six women had their nerves severely tested as they passed through the many crises their prison life inevitably brought. Occasionally one would withdraw from the group for a few days and not take part in their get-togethers, finding being with the others too much of a strain.

∽⬩

MARGRIT: In spite of everything, I felt we coped with the long time together very well. Obviously there were differences of opinion on occasions, and sometimes one or the other would feel the need to avoid certain people. But these conflicts could almost always be resolved.

During our time in the reform school prison, I found the cramped conditions in which we were forced to live and the large number of people a real strain, particularly because it was never quiet. I had absolutely no privacy, not even in the bathroom, which I found really tough. But on the other hand, I learned through it to show particular consideration for others, to pull myself together and not just let myself go. We all had to learn these things; otherwise, we'd just have argued all the time.

In the second prison, when we were by ourselves, life was a lot quieter. Once we'd clarified who was keen to do what and had drawn up clear schedules dividing up our various duties, we found a lot of our wrangling simply disappeared.

KATI: When you live with other people in such close confines for so long, you suddenly find all kinds of things start to annoy you which you'd otherwise barely notice. Sometimes it was really trivial things: the water bottle being left in the wrong place, or something which hadn't been cleared away. I had to guard against allowing frustration or bitterness to build up inside me.

I often had to say, 'Hey guys, I was being silly. I'm really sorry I moaned at you.' And then usually everything was forgotten again.

The biblical principle of asking for, and granting, forgiveness makes it much easier to live together. I don't think ever in my life have I asked others for forgiveness and consciously forgiven others myself as often as I did in those three months. And that applied not only to the other prisoners, but also to the guards and the Taliban as a whole.

A letter from Silke to her friends

25 September 2001

Dear all,

Greetings from my humble cell. It looks like there's a possibility today to smuggle out letters, so I'm seizing the opportunity to write. Who knows, perhaps the odd letter or two will get through.

I am well, considering the circumstances. We are relieved to be deloused and de-wormed and finally have amoebic dysentery behind us as well—for the second time. A week ago we were moved to another prison. This one is Hilton-style compared with the last place. Our guards do their best to fulfil our every wish . . .

The power supply is somewhat precarious—we have a set of naked wires which you're supposed to stick in a broken-off multi-socket plug until you see sparks, by which time you're in business. We get our water from a pump out in the yard, so whenever you use the toilet, you have to be prepared to work a bit first.

All in all life here is very quiet, if not to say boring. Since our diplomats left Afghanistan two weeks ago, our supply of books has dried up. Our activities are now limited to praying, singing and playing cards. Obviously preparing any food takes up a lot of time too—everything has to be washed and disinfected thoroughly.

Spiritually, we are all doing really well. Obviously, we'd

like to see the end of this soon, but we know that we are in God's hands and in the centre of his plan for this country. I have never spent so much time praying as here. We feel very close to God and would not have chosen another way, regardless of how it will end. We have all won a new, much deeper love for this country. The suffering around us is indescribable. So much violence and pain! We almost feel guilty for the preferential treatment we are getting here.

Please pray for the children in our project. They were also arrested and beaten, along with our Afghan staff. The children have allegedly all been released now, but the men are still in prison. They are forced to live under terrible conditions: they spent weeks without seeing daylight, unable to leave their cells or talk to each other. Their only crime is to have worked for Shelter.

Silke

SILKE: Communicating with the outside world was a huge problem. We wrote loads of letters, but very few—as we later discovered—ever reached their destination. We also knew that lots of people were sending us letters, but we only ever received a small number.

Our diplomats and lawyer acted as messengers when they were able to. Once they could no longer visit us, late in October, the lines just went dead. We were totally cut off, always uncertain who knew what and if any news of us had got out at all. Two of us, Margrit and I, had elderly parents and worried in particular about how they were coping with the ordeal.

One of the awful things was that for some time we Germans were purposely denied access to our mail while the Americans and Australians received some letters. One day, a certain Mr Najibullah Khan arrived from the Foreign Ministry—a very unpleasant and cynical man. He had mail which he proceeded to distribute to the Australians and Americans, smiling broadly the whole time.

Once again there was nothing for me—as had been the case for weeks. I lost my composure completely, ran out into the yard and sat on the steps crying uncontrollably. Evidently feeling sorry for me, the prison overseer, Mullah Hamid, tried to console me. But I was in no mood to be comforted.

'Why is it only the others get mail?' I shouted in Pashtu. 'Mr Khan isn't fair to us. The Taliban are all cruel people.'

Mullah Hamid must have worked on Mr Khan considerably, because that same evening this normally very cynical man turned up with a satellite phone and allowed us to call our relatives back home. It was the first time after eight weeks in prison that I had been able to talk to my parents and convince them I was all right and they shouldn't worry excessively.

✧

PETER: It felt like a miracle to be able to talk to my daughter in Australia after so many weeks' isolation, and to assure her that she didn't need to worry too much about me. I was so moved to hear her voice I couldn't hold back the tears.

One of the Taliban laughed at me. 'I didn't know you were such a weakling and would start crying,' he said derisively.

I asked him: 'Do you have a daughter? Do you love her? If you love her then you'll also have feelings for her. If a man cries, then it simply shows he has feelings—powerful feelings. It doesn't mean he's weak.'

He looked at me with a baffled expression, but I think he grasped a little of what I was getting at.

Some of the guards had it in for me anyway because I regularly made a big thing of shaving. 'You're weak like a woman because you don't have a beard,' they would mock.

'How can a beard make you strong?' I would always reply. 'A beard can't make you a real man.'

I think some of them were just jealous, especially the younger ones. I was doing something they weren't allowed to do.

∽

A short while after the aid workers were moved to the intelligence service prison, Peter and Georg were joined by a group of students. The Taliban had arrested them on suspicion of being Massoud sympathisers and working for the Northern Alliance.

One of them, a Pashtun named Mohammed Sharif, spoke very good English. He came from an area of Afghanistan where Shelter Now had set up one of its factories for manufacturing prefabricated concrete sections for housing. Georg had often visited Mohammed's home town and knew many of the people in his tribe.

Mohammed had heard on Radio Sharia that a group of foreigners had been arrested on charges of spreading Christianity. His tribe had immediately thought Shelter Now might be affected and suspected the charges were simply a pretext for the arrests. Now that he had landed in the same prison, he was keen to meet this Mr George who was so highly respected in his tribe.

The two men warmed to each other immediately and spent a lot of time together. Since Mohammed could speak good English, Peter was able to join in their conversations. (Georg spoke with the other inmates in Pashtu, which Peter spoke only haltingly.)

From then on, the three men ate their lunch and evening meals together. This was possible because Mohammed enjoyed something of a special status in the prison, coming as he did from a well-known and powerful tribe. The prison director knew that he would have to answer to the tribe if he started harass- ing Mohammed as he did the other prisoners, so Mohammed was able to spend as much time with Georg as he desired.

He was also not forced to participate in the usual prison chores, and was even able to move freely in the prison office. This meant he could hear the news on the radio and listen in on the conversations of the Taliban guards.

Peter and Georg were very touched by the way Mohammed always took care of them, petitioning the prison directors on their behalf. He helped ensure that they were able to visit their team-mates in the women's prison each day and made sure that no one ever spoke badly of them as foreigners. On some occasions he even managed to secure fewer beatings for his fellow Afghan prisoners. His interventions were risky and at times downright dangerous, but he was backed up by a powerful tribe which was already outraged that its Mr George had been locked up for no reason.

Mohammed was amazed at how well Georg was acquainted with his country and its customs. He wanted to know as much as possible about Georg's life and how his aid organisation had helped other Afghans. As time was hardly an issue, they sat together for hours while Georg answered question after question.

Mohammed Sharif and the other prisoners were deeply impressed by the way Georg and Peter lived out their faith. There was a continual coming and going between the cells, and often some of the inmates would wander into Georg and Peter's cell while they were praying or reading the Bible together. They did this each morning.

'Could you leave us alone for a while?' Georg would say. 'We're just praying.'

Most of the Afghans would then hover in the doorway expecting the prayer to be over in a few minutes. For them, prayer was a ritual which was repeated often but didn't in itself take very long. These foreigners, however, didn't seem to want to stop—and the amount of time they spent reading their holy book! Georg had also decided to fast every Friday, the

Muslim holy day. This practice served only to increase their respect for him.

'You really are devout men,' they would say with genuine approval. 'Not like so many foreigners who don't believe in God and have no holy book.'

Sometimes they would come just to look at Georg's Bible. They were familiar with holy books; Islam in fact teaches that there are four: the Koran, the Torah and the Sabur (the five books of Moses and the Psalms), and the Injil (New Testament). But many had never even seen an Injil and asked Georg whether they might simply hold it for a while. They first went to wash their hands, then took the Bible reverently and pressed it against their chests. Some even kissed it.

At times prisoners asked Georg to read to them from the Bible. They were curious to know what it taught and keen to learn, although they had been instructed by the mullahs that the Christians' holy book had been changed from the original manuscripts. The subject of 'faith' was always discussed at great length. Often the Afghans would leave the room deep in thought.

'How come these foreigners are locked up in here?' many began to ask. 'They respect our Islamic faith and are themselves so devout. And they have helped so many Afghan refugees.'

◈

PETER: Georg spent more time with the other prisoners than I did. He had the major advantage of being good in

At the time of the aid workers' arrest, camps in Pakistan and Afghanistan held over 3.5 million Afghan refugees.

Shelter Now built thousands of clay houses to replace tents for refugee families.

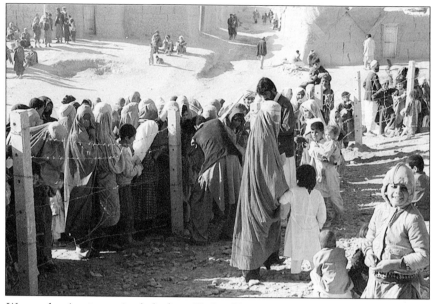
Women hoping to receive help from Shelter Now.

Children are those who suffer most in drought, famine and war.

A young girl fetches water for her family.

In the year 2000, Shelter Now supplied 10,000 families with three quilted blankets each.

Above: A refugee child is pleased to get a new blanket and something to eat.

Left: In 2000, Shelter Now distributed around 13,000 pairs of children's sandals to 4500 families.

A Shelter Now daily drinking water distribution.

One of thousands of wells and irrigation systems (*kareezes*) drilled or repaired by Shelter Now.

Refugee children queue for a daily hot meal.

Shelter Now factories produce concrete
roof beams for building houses since
wood is in very short supply.

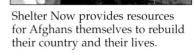

Shelter Now provides resources
for Afghans themselves to rebuild
their country and their lives.

Men building their clay houses.
Each one is approximately 4.5 metres
square, comprising one room and an
adjoining bathroom.

Kati with a group of Kabul street children.

Left: School girls in Kabul after the fall of the Taliban.

Below: One of many schools built by Shelter Now—this one for girls as well as boys.

Bakeries built by Shelter Now enable wheat given as food aid to be turned into bread.

Above: A village health clinic constructed by Shelter Now.

Left: Afghanistan's 10 million uncleared landmines are one of the country's greatest dangers.

Above: Food is distributed at Hope Village, a project begun since Shelter Now personnel returned to Afghanistan.

Right: A new school goes up near Hope Village.

Children are the future of Afghanistan.

Pashtu and of being a very outgoing person. Also, the other men tended to seek him out because in their culture it is natural to cultivate the friendship of the most important man, the leader of the organisation.

But I had some very good relationships with guys who spoke a little English, and ones with whom I could speak my little bit of Dari. Sometimes Georg would interpret for me.

∽⟨⟩

Peter and Georg were also continually receiving reports of what good and devout women their colleagues were. This was partly a result of their singing, which could be heard far away and which all the Afghans knew was worship to God.

But the women's section was also directly beneath the office of the prison management. Mullah Hamid was deeply impressed by the way the women observed Afghan culture in all their behaviour. They would always pull on a headscarf before going out into the courtyard, for example, even if they were only going to collect water. He was taken by the way they always addressed their guards in a polite and restrained manner, speaking not English but Pashtu and a little Dari.

On more than one occasion, he said they were like 'sisters' to him, which was a huge honour coming from an Afghan, indicating that he considered them to be under his special protection.

'They are really devout and honourable women,' he told Georg one day.

Georg's openness towards all the Afghans at the prison and his genuine acts of friendship, coupled with the wise behaviour of the women, slowly earned the aid workers a great deal of respect among both their fellow prisoners and most of their Taliban guards. In this way, the more hardline guards, who hated all Westerners on principle, were forced to be more restrained in their attacks on them.

Their fate may well have been quite different had they not been so familiar with Afghan culture and behaved so wisely.

7

Raining Bombs and Prayers

During their three months in prison, the aid workers celebrated three birthdays. The first was Diana's on 30 August. This was followed by Peter's on 29 September and Dayna's on 4 November. Georg's wife, Marianne, had her birthday on 3 October, and it was celebrated somewhat wistfully in her absence.

For Peter, as for the other two, that year's birthday was one he is unlikely to forget.

PETER: With the monotony of prison life, I never thought that my birthday would turn out to be such a huge celebration. But Georg managed to order an enormous birthday cake for me—three tiers, no less! It was very impressive.

My first thought was, *Who's going to eat it all?* But in the afternoon we had a party with all the prisoners in our wing and they each had a piece. There was enough for the guards to get generous portions as well.

During the party, Georg gave a birthday speech, doling out lavish praise for me and my work. I would normally have been embarrassed by such things, but under the circumstances it was somehow fitting. He spoke of how I had come to Afghanistan to help the people there.

'Mr Peter is an engineer,' he explained. 'He repaired hundreds of wells in the Ghazni region. He was also responsible for building a clinic in Logar and headed up another project in which thousands of wells were cleaned and repaired.'

The Afghans whispered approvingly among themselves. Some then gave short speeches, including one older gentleman with a white flowing beard, a highly respected general. 'We are grateful to you *khaarijees* [foreigners] for coming to our country and doing so much good for our people,' he said. 'We are very saddened that you are here in prison. We hope and pray that you will soon be released and reunited with your families. We appreciate and respect you greatly.'

I will always cherish the memory of that party with the prisoners and guards. It was one of the most outstanding experiences of my life.

Later that day, we were also able to meet with the women and enjoyed another party among ourselves.

GEORG: Marianne's birthday was a more melancholy occasion. Fortunately I had at least managed to send her a letter via our Pakistani lawyer quite a while earlier. And Silke, our resident artist, had painted a beautiful card in which we were all able to write a personal message. Once that had been done, all I could do was hope against hope that it would reach her in time for her birthday.

For me personally, the most difficult and painful aspect

of my imprisonment was the separation from Marianne and my children.

As soon as I awoke that morning, my thoughts flew to my wife. I was racked with pain. What would she be thinking and going through now? What would she be feeling? Would she have enough faith to take her through and not begin to doubt? What I would have given to be allowed to talk to her!

I had ordered a huge birthday cake from the market with 'Happy Birthday Marianne' written on it, and in the afternoon we were given permission to go to the women's prison and hold a small party with the others. They had brewed up a big pot of coffee and we proceeded to carve up the cake. We celebrated as best we could and as much as our feelings would allow. The others then prayed for Marianne and for me, which was a particular comfort. In the end I was able to find that inner balance. At the same time, I hoped desperately that Marianne had enjoyed her birthday in spite of the pain of our separation.

Later I discovered that our birthday card and letter had reached her in time and had been a great comfort to her.

❧

One day some of the other prisoners came to Georg saying they had heard that his sixteen Afghan staff were being held in the same prison. 'They're in two cells, one facing the inner courtyard, the other looking out of the back of the building,' he was told.

After that Georg began to use his daily walks in the courtyard to scan all the barred windows, straining to look inside. One afternoon he thought he caught a

A letter from Georg to Udo Stolte, Director of Shelter Germany

Kabul, 3 October 2001

Dear Udo,

Greetings from Kabul. Tomorrow somebody is leaving the prison and has agreed to take this letter with them. I felt it was a good opportunity to update you on our situation. When we send letters officially, we are only allowed to write how well we are, that everything is okay etc. I once complained about the state of the toilets here and the next day the boss came by and was very cross with me. He is incredibly brutal and in charge of all the interrogations here.

All the prisoners are beaten with steel cables and others undergo torture. About two hours ago, four inmates walked past us in the corridor in a terrible state: their hands and feet were all swollen and they could hardly walk. It looked awful. That is our current environment—horror is ever-present. Little wonder that I can hardly sleep at night. Sometimes I take high dosages of sleeping pills to help me . . .

The situation in Kabul has deteriorated. There have been a number of anti-American demonstrations. We could hear the people shouting on the streets from our prison. The demonstrators then burned down part of the American embassy. One of the high-level officials from our prison was among the crowd.

We were extremely afraid during the demonstration and prayed a lot. Our guards would certainly have made no attempt to protect us had the mob decided to storm our prison.

Thankfully, we have not yet been in any life-threatening situations. If the United States were to launch a full-scale attack, all hell would break loose here. We're praying with everything we've got that we'll be free before things really get going here. Some of the team are already close to breaking point. We really need a miracle . . .

We have often felt we were at the end of ourselves, unable to hold out another day. But God has continually given us new strength to carry on . . . We have a strong suspicion that most people have no idea of what we are going through. We often only pass on the more positive things so that our relatives won't worry about us even more.

Your close friend,
Georg

glimpse of the face of Gul Khan, his project manager, at one of the windows. He wandered a little closer, always keeping an eye out to ensure the guards were not observing him. This time two figures appeared for a brief moment at the barred window.

Georg casually lifted a hand and gave them a quick wave. A flash of recognition in the eyes and a strained smile told him he had made contact.

From then on, Peter and Georg made a point of walking past that window every afternoon. Each time one or another of their staff would appear and wave briefly.

Georg discovered the second cell one evening almost by accident. He was looking out of his window when suddenly he heard familiar voices. His eyes strayed over the lit windows of the next wing, and there he spied one of his staff members. He waved tirelessly until he finally attracted his attention.

All eight men then stepped up to the window in turn to wave to him and Peter, who had immediately rushed to the window too. The two men had to fight back tears. From that day on, several of the men would come to the window each evening and wave to them.

As a rule, a selected prisoner would be posted as guard in each wing of the prison. Georg was able to win over one of these guards, who then agreed to pass on a brief note to his staff.

'I am so sorry that you are having to suffer because of us,' Georg wrote. 'Please don't worry about your families. Our staff at the Peshawar office are providing for them.'

The sixteen Afghan staff were being held in the strictest conditions and subjected to gruelling interrogations and beatings. The Taliban used these methods to try to extract false confessions that they had been talked into converting to Christianity or bribed in some other way. But not one of them gave in or spoke against his employers.

Georg wrote to Udo Stolte: 'They're being treated like saboteurs, mass murderers and hardened criminals. It's absolutely crazy and totally unjust! When I tried to speak on their behalf I was pushed aside with a brusque: "They're bad criminals." '

One morning, Peter and Georg were looking out their cell window when they noticed an old prison bus pull up. They were just in time to see their sixteen staff members bundled into the vehicle and driven away. Through the internal information channels, they learned that they had been taken to the infamous Pul-e-Tsharki prison to join around 6000 other inmates.

There they remained until 13 November, when their guards fled from approaching Northern Alliance troops and they, along with all the other inmates, were able to walk out of the prison. In this way, the eight aid workers, who always feared their employees might be executed, received the answer to their almost daily prayer: 'God, if you free us from the Taliban, please rescue our Afghan staff first.'

Shelter Now saw to the welfare of the Afghan employees' families from its base in Pakistan. The team members in Peshawar provided accommodation for the workers' relatives who had fled to Pakistan, and the organisation continued to pay the men's wages to their families.

Although all of Shelter Now's aid projects in Afghanistan were stopped following the arrests, its refugee camps in Pakistan continued to run as normal, thanks to the efforts of the agency's local staff. In some cases, operations were even stepped up.

When Shelter Now's sixteen Afghan employees were released from prison in Kabul, all of them expressed the desire to continue working with the organisation.

The first outward sign of war came on Sunday afternoon, 7 October. Georg and Peter were taking their usual stroll in the prison courtyard when the whole of Kabul suddenly erupted in gunfire. It was mostly anti-aircraft fire, but individual Kalashnikovs were also clearly audible.

A single small aircraft was circling over the city—evidently a reconnaissance plane.

It seemed a pointless waste of ammunition, but for the Taliban it was probably a chance to vent some of the tension that had been building up for weeks. They were expecting the United States to strike at any moment. Day by day, the enemy was closing in. Troops were stationed in Pakistan and Tajikistan. Aircraft carriers were anchored in the Indian Ocean, ready for action at a moment's notice. But no one knew when, where or how severely the foreign troops would strike. The whole country was holding its breath in fear and trepidation.

In the end, the 'global coalition against terror' took a full four and a half weeks to prepare its attack—a nerve-racking time for the Taliban.

◈

GEORG: As soon as the shooting started, I asked to go over and see the women. Fortunately permission was given.

'Don't worry. The US haven't started their bombing yet,' I told them quickly. 'There's just a spy drone circling up there and the Taliban are going mad. But things could get started for real tonight. Why don't we pray together that God will protect us, and that the Americans will somehow find out where we are?'

We had received a reliable tip-off that the US forces knew our location and would try to avoid us in their raids.

As I had predicted, the bombing began that night, targeting selected objects in Kabul. During this time, Peter and I were locked up with the other male prisoners on the first floor. If the prison had been hit, none of us would have survived. Nevertheless, our Afghan inmates were more excited than afraid: the war improved their chances of release.

'We pray to Allah five times a day that this regime will be toppled,' I was told repeatedly.

The impact of the bombs and the subsequent explosions broke in waves over the city. Lights flashed across the sky. The pounding was so great that the walls of the prison shook. We ran from one side of the window to the other, observing the scene around us.

The second night was worse still as the jets picked out targets closer to the prison. The noise was incredible. The walls quaked so badly I was left gasping with shock. I looked at the barricaded steel door and remembered there was no escape. We were caged up with nowhere to run, and it could all explode any second.

We knew that one major target had been hit nearby— our whole building rocked as if there had been an earthquake. The sky outside our window lit up like day. The next day I learned that the Radio Sharia tower, right near the prison, had been taken out by a single bomb.

During another night raid, the radar equipment and television tower were blown away. The tower was one of Kabul's landmarks, positioned on a mountain where it rose up proudly over the city. When we looked out of our window the next morning, no tower or radar could be seen. The top of the mountain had been cut clean away.

We later heard through a foreign radio station that this feat had earned the female pilot personal recognition from President Bush. For the Taliban, it was particularly galling that a woman had been the author of such destruction. Women in Kabul weren't even allowed to drive cars, but this one had flown over the city and obliterated one of its key installations.

<hr>

The bombing campaign was one of the severest tests the aid workers went through. At times the tension was so great that one or the other would go to pieces and begin screaming or beating the wall in fear or frustration, refusing to be comforted or pacified by the others.

<hr>

KATI: I didn't find the first night of bombing so bad. Experiencing the sudden racket of the anti-aircraft fire that afternoon had in a way prepared me for what was coming. Georg and Peter had also come over to explain what was happening.

The evening raid began with signal rockets, which quite reminded me of the New Year firework displays back home. In the end, we decided to go outside and watch the show. The real raid didn't begin until later that night, when we were already asleep.

But the second night was really extreme. The bombs

started dropping right near the prison. All of us, except Silke, moved into the hall away from any windows which we feared would shatter. I was petrified.

Before every bomb we would hear a whistling sound followed by a deafening explosion. The floor would shake violently and my stomach would cramp right up. At night it's worse than in the day because you can't see what's going on. Again and again I prayed, 'Lord, please protect us and bring us out of here safely.'

Later on I started to get used to the bombing and sometimes even slept right through it. But when I was awake, I sometimes asked myself: *Why am I afraid?* I wasn't so much scared of death itself because then I would be with God and everything would be fine. Basically it was the unpredictability of our situation which made me afraid. To hear a fighter jet somewhere nearby and know that a bomb was about to drop, and yet to have that terrible uncertainty: where would it hit? Perhaps our prison?

Even now, I hate the memory of those jets and the whistling noise before impact.

❦

DIANA: The night the bombing started we all slept in the hallway. But I only slept there one or two days—the mice were too bad. I got the idea of putting sticky tape all over our glass window so that the glass wouldn't shatter. Then we slowly moved back in.

After that, most of us slept in our room. When we heard a plane overhead we would quickly open the window so the glass wouldn't break.

✄

MARGRIT: The first night I lay down with the others in the hall and looked at the walls, which were already cracked almost from top to bottom. I decided that it wouldn't actually take a direct hit for our prison to collapse. Just one thorough shake and the whole thing was sure to come down like a pack of cards.

The bombs continued to explode, some right in our vicinity. I was seized by panic. 'O God, what should I do?' I cried out inside. 'I can't run away! I can't get out!'

At that moment it was as though someone nudged me and said: 'Stay calm. Just turn over and go to sleep. Everything's going to be okay.'

God was there with me the whole night. I felt so moved. I am utterly convinced that it is not possible to simply imagine such a thing. Either you experience it and are therefore able to stay calm, or you go mad.

✄

PETER: An intelligence service building such as the one we were held in would normally be a target in a war, but I didn't feel unprotected. I think this was for two reasons. The main one was that I felt God was looking after us. The other was that we had reason to believe the Americans had been told where we were.

I could also see, very early in the piece, the accuracy of the bombing, so I wasn't terribly worried.

It sounds strange to say this when some of the bombs were falling quite close—we could see and hear them exploding—but I was more comforted by the bombing than afraid of it. I knew what it meant in terms of getting rid of the Taliban.

Letters from Diana to her sister Josephine

3 October

Dear Josephine,

When we come out we don't know what will be left of our possessions. We have been told that our houses have been given over to our landlords; that means we may have lost everything . . .

We have also heard that the team in Peshawar have all left. Don't know what to expect once we come out. Your support is much required in this area!

Love and hugs to Mum and Dad and everyone else.

14 October

I hope you got my last message. I don't know if things are getting to you or not . . . Don't know how long we are here. More delays! Our times are in God's hands.

The bombs and missiles started seven nights ago. Nightly the attacks continue. All the city is darkened at 7.30 p.m. so we sit in darkness and have praise and worship and intercession [prayer]. Please pray for our safe release as we fear a backlash as we are the only foreigners in this country.

We still have an overwhelming peace. Our work in Afghanistan has been destroyed. Much love always.

Diana

The day of release for Georg and Peter's friend
Mohammed Sharif and the other Afghan students
came more quickly than anyone expected. Normally
prisoners disappeared without any great farewells,
overjoyed to be able to leave prison life behind them.
But Mohammed did not look at all happy when he
learned he was about to be set free.

He went straight to Georg. 'I've been given my
release papers but I'm not leaving,' he announced.
'I'm going to stay here with you until you're finally
freed. I've spoken to my father and grandfather and
they are in agreement, although they would of course
like to have me home.'

This was around the middle of October. Mohammed's decision was particularly courageous in view of
the US bombing campaign, which had been stepped
up in recent days. What with the air raids on Kabul
and the frontline between Northern Alliance and
Taliban troops now only 30 kilometres north of the
city, Kabul had become a dangerous place to be. Many
who had not already gone were now leaving, seeking
refuge in the countryside.

Mohammed had no way of knowing how long it
would be before the Shelter Now team were free.

Georg and Peter were deeply moved by Mohammed's costly display of friendship. Their fellow inmates
were also impressed. 'Thank you, my friend,' said
Georg. 'Thank you for your friendship. I know there are
more Afghans who love us than those who want to
harm us.'

Over the next few weeks, Mohammed's presence was extremely helpful. He continued to carry messages for the aid workers and kept them supplied with the latest news from the prison office radio. His presence also helped Georg and Peter to deepen their friendships with some of the prison guards.

❧

The allied forces spent several weeks strategically targeting and destroying the most important military installations. After that, they turned their attention to the frontline between the Taliban and Northern Alliance fighters, which by that time was about 30 kilometres north of Kabul in the region of Shamali. The aid workers heard fighter jets roar over the prison and a short while later the distant pounding of bombs as they hit their targets.

The Taliban in Kabul were particularly appalled by the way in which a plane would suddenly appear from nowhere, take out a single building and then immediately disappear again. The precision with which the individual groups of leading Taliban were eliminated stunned them and spread a sense of helplessness and fear.

Not surprisingly, the aggression of some Taliban guards towards the eight Westerners soon began to increase. Peter and Georg in particular found themselves on the receiving end. One of their guards once remarked: 'If we're forced to flee, we'll kill all the foreigners first.'

A few guards even began referring to 'Mr George' malevolently as 'Bush'.

Some nights, Georg and Peter found it hard to sleep, knowing that the harder the Taliban were hit, the more precarious their own situation became. Georg compared some of their captors to wild animals—the worse their wounds, the more unpredictable their behaviour.

On days following a particularly destructive night of bombing, the two men decided to play safe and not go out for their daily walk in the prison courtyard, where the Taliban may have been tempted to vent their aggression on them.

The prison overseer, Mullah Hamid, who had grown genuinely fond of the eight foreigners, became extremely concerned for their safety. On more than one occasion he said to Georg anxiously, 'Mr George, I'm worried that the Taliban in Kandahar or al-Qaeda fighters might abduct you as hostages or kill you in revenge. I don't know how I can protect you.'

Unfortunately, Mullah Hamid's superior, Mullah Yusuf, was not at all well-disposed to the detainees. He was an unscrupulous man who rarely came into the prison, but when he did he made it his business to make life hard for the Afghan inmates.

One morning Peter and Georg were summoned to the office of the prison director. They arrived to find a group of Taliban sitting in a kind of conservatory designed to receive special delegations. Mullah Yusuf was there, flanked by another very important-looking mullah with an extremely large turban. Four or five other Taliban completed the group. Georg had never seen any of the men before. They eyed the two Westerners closely, asked them a few questions and then proceeded to talk among themselves in Dari rather than Pashtu so that Georg could not understand. Finally they stood up and left.

These forbidding characters instilled in Georg a deep sense of fear. As it turned out, it was justified. One of their more friendly guards later told Georg that the delegation had come from Kandahar. This confirmed his suspicions that the aid workers were in great danger of being dragged off to the Taliban's southern stronghold as hostages.

∽

In the evening of 21 October (the day Atif Ali Khan returned from Pakistan to try to get an answer from the Supreme Court), Georg and Peter were just getting ready for bed when Georg was summoned to the prison office. Somewhat perturbed, he followed the guard down the dark hallway.

In the office he found the overseer, Mullah Hamid, along with Mullah Yusuf. Typically, Yusuf wasted no time with niceties.

'Pack your things—you're both being moved for the night,' he ordered.

There it was again, the surprise tactics designed to unnerve the prisoners. Georg had to fight to pull himself together and not reveal his fear.

Excerpts from two letters written home

21 October 2001

Dear Sabine and Armin,

I wonder if you've received any of my previous letters.

The situation here has changed dramatically, as you will no doubt be aware. To tell you the truth, we are really in danger. But I am still confident that we'll be out of here soon.

I would never have thought that I would hold up so well in a war situation. Being in prison obviously makes things much worse because you can't run away. We can't see what's going on either; we just hear the blasts all the time. The noise at night is often unbearable. Sometimes I lie in bed just waiting for the next bomb and hoping that it won't hit the prison.

But I'm amazed that I feel so much at peace in spite of everything. I hardly feel afraid at all. My faith gives me a lot of strength. But still I wish I could leave here right now. It's very hard.

Often we sleep in the inner corridor at night in case the glass in the windows of our cell shatters in the bombing. But we're not alone. We share the establishment with whole armies of cockroaches, spiders and other wildlife. It's amazing what you can get used to.

Margrit

20 October 2001

Dear Udo,

So far, we've managed to survive all the air raids with our nerves still intact. Since yesterday, everything has been quiet . . .

The atmosphere is growing increasingly tense. More and more we find ourselves having to really focus on God and his promises; we wouldn't cope otherwise. Humanly speaking, our prospects are now extremely bleak. The court proceedings have no doubt been thrown overboard. There are hardly any high-level Taliban left here now. Most of them have fled south. Only the less important people have stayed behind . . .

We don't receive any faxes or other messages anymore: all the staff at the Foreign Ministry who used to bring us the faxes appear to have fled. It's very discouraging. The incessant bombing, the tension and the uncertainty of everything are an incredible challenge. It's now perfectly clear to us that we're being held here as hostages—by people who hate us . . .

Georg

'Why do we have to leave here?' he protested.

'We're taking you to a better place,' came the all-too-familiar reply. 'It's safer there, particularly during these night bombing raids.'

Georg didn't believe a word of it. 'We don't need a better place. It's fine here, and we want to stay.'

Mullah Yusuf became aggressive. 'Who's the boss around here? Who gives the orders—you or me?'

'You, of course.'

'Then get your things and see to it that you're back here quickly!'

Georg saw he had no choice. Reluctantly, he went off to tell Peter the bad news. The two quickly packed a few things and then padlocked their cell door from the outside. They walked back down the corridor, full of foreboding and wondering: *What are they up to now?*

Strangely enough, the prison had become a home to them over the previous five weeks. They had built up friendships with prisoners and got to know the guards. The system was familiar—to a certain extent it even felt safe. Their Afghan fellow prisoners had often volunteered to protect them should any radical Taliban storm the prison. Some even declared that if they were freed by the Northern Alliance, they would hide the foreigners in their homes until it was safe for them to leave.

The Afghans were as dismayed as Peter and Georg by this latest development, especially their friend Mohammed Sharif. He walked partway down the corridor with them before coming to a stop, his shoulders slumped. He was powerless to help them.

Once again their future was uncertain and dangerous. They were hostages without rights, without support.

When the two men climbed into the waiting van outside, the six women were already seated. Their faces told the same tale of dismay. Like Peter and Georg, they did not believe they would return in the morning, as their guards had told them. They had decided to bring all their scanty belongings with them just in case.

As Georg was the one most familiar with the area, he again made a point of memorising the route taken by the convoy. Their journey took them through the centre of the city, past the Turkish embassy and then on to the Chinese embassy. Finally they rounded a bend and drew up next to the former East German embassy, outside one of the intelligence service's high-security prisons—the infamous Riasat 3.

As soon as they climbed out of the van, they were separated again. The women were deposited on the first floor of the building while the men were taken down to the basement.

GEORG: Peter and I were led along a dark corridor. At the end was a large metal door which opened onto steps leading down into the basement. There we found the worst conditions I have ever seen. Prisoners with sad or expressionless faces shuffled past us. Many were visibly traumatised or mentally disturbed: their faces twitched, their eyes were empty.

We had entered a world of no hope, and it took my breath away.

Words can barely describe the atmosphere. The air was damp and cold. Many of the men were ill and clearly in shock. I was accustomed to a lot, but being in an underground cell brought on my first ever attack of claustrophobia.

A single shaft of light came from just below the ceiling, through an opening that looked out onto the ground one metre below street level.

Peter and I sat down on our mattresses stunned and speechless. We must have looked rather like the other prisoners staring back at us.

Two of the inmates who weren't quite so far gone evidently saw how shocked we were and did their best to help us. The first one introduced himself as Mustafa. He turned out to be a very bright individual with whom I quickly became friends. He made us some tea and described the prison to us.

'Kabul has Riasat 1 right through to Riasat 12,' he said. 'Lots of the prisoners here have been sentenced to death. Others are waiting for amputations. Most of them are quite innocent. Very few have ever committed any real crime. This prison has another wing which is much worse than this one here.'

Peter and I were in despair. We sat in our cell not knowing what to say.

Fortunately, we had received letters from Atif just before being moved from the other prison. *I'll start by reading my letters*, I thought, hoping this would help take my mind off things.

There were several from Marianne, who I had recently learned was now even further away from me—in Germany. Before I had assumed she and the children were still in Pakistan, but they had left because of the volatile situation there. As I sat thinking about the distance between us, I was overcome with wretchedness.

Finally, I picked up the letters and began to read. In the first one, Marianne wrote that her father had had an accident. By the second one, he was in a coma. By the third, he had died and the funeral had already been held.

How had Marianne got through it all? How had she managed to comfort her mother? And our boys—for them it was the first time that an immediate relative had died.

What thoughts had been going through their minds during the funeral when they thought of their own father?

It was the final straw. I felt absolutely lost. I flipped open my Bible and started reading. I came to Psalm 91: 'You will not fear the terror of night . . . because you have made the Lord your refuge . . . For he will command his angels concerning you to guard you in all your ways.' The words washed over me like waves of comfort. I read them again and again. Peter and I then prayed together for our families, pouring our hearts out to God.

That night I could not sleep, despite taking two sleeping tablets. The sounds and smells in the prison were so alien and sinister. On our arrival, I had noticed with horror that some of the prisoners wore thick heavy chains. As I dozed fretfully in and out of sleep, I was haunted by the jangling and scraping of shackles as inmates shuffled along the corridor.

❦

Eventually morning came. The hours dragged on, but nobody came to collect them.

Have the Taliban lied to us again? they wondered. *We were only supposed to be here overnight. Do we really have to stay?*

The pair paced nervously up and down the corridor outside their cell. 'O God, get us out of here,' they prayed in despair. 'We can't cope with this terrible place. We'll go mad like the others if we have to stay here. Please give the Taliban a change of heart and make them decide to come and fetch us.'

At around 11.00 a.m. guards finally came, telling them curtly, 'Get your things and come with us.'

For Georg and Peter, it was almost as good as being released. Taken back to their old prison, together with the women, they were greeted by the Afghan prisoners crowding round them, overjoyed to have them back. It was like coming home.

Mohammed Sharif told Georg that early that morning guards had tried to break into their cell to get their things. But they had not been able to smash the lock. Georg thought they had probably intended to take his and Peter's few belongings to them at the other prison. Later, the Afghan prisoners had heard the guards arguing about what to do with the foreigners. It was then that they had suddenly decided to fetch them back. For Georg and Peter, it was a clear answer to their fervent prayers that morning.

From that time on, the eight aid workers often spent the night at the high-security Riasat 3. For a while they were taken there every night, and then sometimes only every second or third night. They would be collected around six o'clock in the evening and brought back around seven next morning.

They could only guess why this was done. One reason may have been that Riasat 3 was safer during the night raids. But it was also quite possible that the Taliban feared the US Special Forces might try to break into the intelligence service prison and free them.

MARGRIT: Riasat 3 was an all-male prison. During the nights we spent there, we were the only women and were held on the first floor. It was actually an office area, sectioned off by a huge barred gate. We were given two rooms: a small one for Silke and Kati and a larger one for the rest of us.

By now it was late October and the nights were bitterly cold. The windows were all broken, and the plastic sheeting that had been fixed up in their place did little to keep out the chill.

A male guard sat permanently in the corridor outside our room, which we found outrageous for Afghanistan.

The whole building had a very eerie atmosphere. I was unable to sleep at night. Bats flew around our window screeching to one another. It's hard to describe the noise they make: one moment it sounded like a baby crying and the next it turned into a nasty, high-pitched scream.

We felt extremely vulnerable being on the first floor during the air raids. If the building had been hit, we would have had no chance of escape. But then, the thought of sleeping below ground like Georg and Peter filled me with dread as well.

DIANA: The Taliban said the night prison would be safer, but it didn't feel safer to us women. We didn't have a female warden and the men tried to come into our room. Men were everywhere, and we absolutely hated it.

We complained vigorously about being taken there, but we couldn't get the Taliban to change their minds.

Eventually we succeeded in getting them to give us a padlock so we could lock our door from the inside.

Once the prison director came into our room with a video camera, wanting to film us. I think he wanted to sell the footage to al-Jazeera and make some money. We refused to let him.

Letter from Diana to her church in Perth

22 October

Dear John [Pastor John Finkelde] and my Hepburn Heights family,

I am always encouraged by your emails. Please don't stop! I need to hear from you and others. Many things I sent did not get thru. We can only trust our lawyer to deliver our messages, and he can only do it when he gets out to Islamabad so it is not very often . . .

Complete climatic change is certainly needed for this devastated nation . . . [God] gives us strength. Now in our third prison, not allowed out of our room . . . The prayers of people around the world are our strength. We need your prayers like never before that we will all come out safe and unharmed. Sometimes we wake up and say this can't be true that we are in prison and are now hostages. After eleven weeks it gets a bit trying, but He is good to us and we hold on to Psalm 91 . . .

I love you all. Your prayers do make a difference.

Diana

When Georg and Peter arrived at Riasat 3 on subsequent evenings, their new friends were already waiting for them. As soon as he heard their vehicle arriving, Mustafa would start making tea. They would sit and talk together until late into the night.

⤫

GEORG: Two weeks passed before I could pluck up the courage to explore the rest of our prison wing. Immediately left of the stairs coming down into the basement, a dark corridor sloped away further underground. Only once did I dare to go down there. I discovered six prisoners crammed into each small cell. Makeshift bunks lined the walls, with a small hatch in the ceiling to let in a few token rays of light. Most of the time, though, it was pitch dark, and power cuts were frequent.

I wondered how the men coped in these dungeons for months on end. Many of them coughed continually owing to the damp air; some had tuberculosis.

There were other cells, housing three men each. They were only allowed out briefly each morning and evening to go to the toilet. Many had their feet in chains so that they could only shuffle along painfully. The chains around their ankles were fitted with another chain which they could hold in each hand. They were supposed to pull this chain upwards when walking to make it easier to drag their feet along and prevent the chain scraping so badly on the ground. The whole scene was reminiscent of a medieval dungeon.

My friend in the intelligence prison, Mohammed Sharif, had earlier brought me a little radio with headphones from the market. I kept this with me the whole time, carefully concealed under my clothing. Each day when we arrived at the night prison, we locked ourselves in our cell with Mustafa and secretly listened to the news from foreign broadcasters. We had to be extremely careful because the Taliban had their spies even among the prisoners.

Mustafa had previously served in the army and was therefore very familiar with the geography of Afghanistan. He explained to us exactly where the fighting was going on and which cities had already fallen to the Northern Alliance, backed up by US forces. He drew a map of Afghanistan, marking the individual towns and cities and explaining developments in the war. The capture of the northern city of Mazar-i-Sharif on 9 November after fierce fighting proved to be a decisive victory for the anti-Taliban alliance. From then on, their progress southwards was rapid.

The following night, we heard that the next town had fallen, followed by another, and another. Within a few days, the Taliban had lost almost the entire north of the country as far as the city of Herat. Each night we sat over the radio spellbound as news came in of the latest victory. By the time the frontline reached Shamali just north of Kabul, we were certain that the liberation of the capital could only be days away.

Each night I would make notes of the news and slip them to the women on the way back to our day prison. After breakfast, the women could then read their 'newspaper'.

A few days later, a commotion suddenly erupted late in the afternoon at the day prison. Guards were running all over the place in great agitation. They were aggressive and the atmosphere was tense.

Peter and Georg were supposed to be receiving soup which the women had made and were about to send over. Mullah Hamid and Mullah Yusuf burst into their cell telling them to get up. 'We're taking you to the night prison immediately!' they barked.

'Why the rush? We haven't even eaten yet.'

'Then take your soup with you! We're leaving *now!*'

They scrambled to their feet and were hurriedly packed off to the night prison, together with the women. Once there, Peter and Georg stumbled down the steps to their basement dungeon where an excited Mustafa was already awaiting them.

'It's happening,' he told them. 'I heard on the news this afternoon that Northern Alliance troops have begun their attack on the frontlines at Shamali and are now heading for Kabul. They're only about six miles away. It can't be long now.'

The prisoners were in a state of great agitation. Anxiously they paced up and down the corridors. No one knew how the events would turn out. Would they be freed by the Northern Alliance, or would their Taliban guards kill them all first? And what would happen to the aid workers?

Just a few short hours later, with the sound of gunfire from outside echoing around the prison, the Taliban seized the prisoners from their cells, loaded them into a Land Cruiser and drove out into the Kabul night, bound for Kandahar.

8

The Streets of Ghazni

Followed by a second Land Cruiser, the vehicle carrying the aid workers raced out of the city. The road was full of Taliban fleeing Kabul. Every vehicle was full to bursting with armed men. It was amazing how many people suddenly couldn't wait to get out of the capital.

The aid workers caught sight of several tanks heading south. The incessant air raids had evidently worn these fighters down to such an extent that now in desperation they were seeking the open country-side.

Travelling at breakneck speed, the two Land Cruisers flew past them all.

GEORG: After about an hour we turned off the road down a steep slope to a village. Mullah Hassan Jashim, the director of Riasat 3, was waiting for us.

Aha! So things must have got a little too hot for you in Kabul, that you felt you had to clear out without us, I thought to myself.

Mullah Hassan climbed into the second vehicle and I

began to feel very uneasy. In fact, I was petrified. I wouldn't put anything past this man. In the night prison he had the reputation of being particularly cruel, personally beating and torturing prisoners at will. He had never beaten us, but he had always been extremely gruff and rude in all our dealings with him. The fact that he was taking charge of us personally was not a good sign.

❧

Georg had good reason to be fearful. In the second Land Cruiser were two Afghan prisoners who had also been taken from Riasat 3. One of these had helped Georg and Peter a great deal while they were there. Now they heard the Taliban discussing what to do with the aid workers.

'Let's kill them all because they are infidels,' said one. 'Then we will become *ghazis*.' *Ghazi* is the religious title for someone who kills an infidel.

'No,' said Mullah Hassan, 'let's take the six women and divide them among us as *ghanimat* [the permitted spoils of holy war]. Let's just kill Peter and Georg.'

The two prisoners listened to this debate with horror. Later they escaped, and Georg subsequently had several meetings with them when they related this story.

❧

GEORG: We sped on past numerous darkened villages for another two or three hours. Again and again we had to stop at checkpoints and roadblocks. And every time I hoped that someone would see that we were foreigners and maybe even come to our rescue.

After his release, Georg discovered that a number of well-meaning Afghans had been keeping an eye on the prison in Kabul and knew the aid workers had been taken away. They caught sight of the foreigners during their journey to Kandahar. A group of about twenty or thirty had set up their own checkpoint, hoping to shoot the Taliban when they arrived and free the team.

But the plan never worked out. Either they set up their checkpoint when the aid workers had already passed, or they failed to recognise them when they turned up. This is possible as the six women were wearing Afghan dress. In retrospect, the eight were glad the plan had failed as it would inevitably have involved a terrible bloodbath.

GEORG: I didn't understand anything anymore. Panic crept over me. My worst fears had come true. Beside me, Peter also seemed to be in shock. He didn't say a single word throughout the entire journey.

I could hardly move on the narrow seat. My legs gradually went to sleep. We were being continually thrown around owing to the poor state of the roads. It was a living nightmare.

As we continued to veer all over the place, Heather suddenly pulled out her little torch and began reading from the

Bible. Among many other verses, she read again and again from Psalm 118: 'I will not die but live, and tell of the works of God.'

We let the words sink in and slowly our rolling prison seemed to fill with peace.

◆

DIANA: After Georg realised we were on the road to Kandahar, I thought: *What's going to happen to us now? Here we are on the road, the bombs are falling and the Americans have no idea where we are.*

Suddenly, bumping along in that vehicle, I felt God say to me, 'Your mission in Kabul is completed.' We later learned that Kabul fell an hour after we were taken out.

Well, what's our mission now, I wondered. *Here we are going to Kandahar: are we going to end up with Mullah Omar and Osama bin Laden?*

The Talib behind the wheel was driving like a maniac, swerving from side to side all over the road. At one stage he turned off his headlights—they seemed to think America needed lights to bomb.

And I kept praying: 'God, you've kept us alive for three-and-a-half months. Are we going to die now?'

◆

KATI: At first I thought we were just being transferred to another prison. But when the Land Cruiser actually drove out of the city, I started to feel really afraid. *What happens if we get caught up between the two fronts and end up in the middle of a wild shoot-out?* I thought.

When Heather began to read verses out of the Bible and we sang the songs we had composed ourselves while in prison, I was amazed that none of the Taliban tried to stop us. I can still remember how my panic turned into an inner calm, more intense than I had ever experienced before. It was basically what is described in the Bible as a peace that passes all understanding. It was so real it was almost tangible.

Suddenly I realised: God is still there! I don't have to worry! He'll have a solution.

❧

PETER: When we started singing the driver turned up the car radio, trying to drown us out. We sang louder and he turned it up louder.

Incredibly, no one told us to be quiet. It was the same in prison—they never stopped us from praying or from praising and worshipping the Lord. Yet, in a way, that was supposed to be the thing we were in jail for!

❧

GEORG: At about 1.00 a.m., the convoy turned off the main road and entered a village. Small clay houses crouched behind high walls. *Finally we're stopping for a rest and we'll be able to spend the night in a house*, I thought to myself.

I stretched my legs and got ready to get out. But no, the vehicle bumped on past the houses towards a rusty, battered steel container in the middle of the open countryside. It was the kind normally used to transport large volumes of goods overseas. We froze with horror at the sight of it.

'We can't possibly go in there. We won't survive it!' some of us protested in complete panic.

Driving through Kabul's outlying districts, it is impossible to miss the steel containers lying abandoned at the side of the road. Some are riddled with bullet holes, others swollen like distorted balloons.

Before the days of the Taliban, the Mujahedin often disposed of their opponents—and any civilians they took a dislike to—by driving them into these containers. Just before they shut the door, they threw a hand grenade inside.

This bestial practice had been continued by the Taliban, as several of the aid workers knew only too well.

GEORG: I tried to reason with the guards. 'Please let us stay in one of the houses. Don't do this to us. Have you no mercy?'

But they refused to be moved. I negotiated with them to at least let us leave the door open. Fortunately they did allow that, but we knew we couldn't trust them. So Heather decided to position herself in the entrance. No amount of persuasion or force could make her budge one centimetre back into the container.

Inside there were a few dirty mattresses and tattered blankets. It was good that we had at least brought a few of our own blankets as the night was bitterly cold.

The entire scene was bizarre and eerie. In the darkness, Heather sat debating with an armed guard in the doorway

to stop herself falling asleep. Outside, strange men appeared
to just hang around.

'Where can we go to the toilet?' asked Margrit. Without
speaking, the guards motioned to the open wasteland. So
the women were forced to relieve themselves as discreetly
as possible while the gathering of intrigued men looked on.
The whole things was beneath human dignity.

For most of us it was a terrible night. Sleep was the last
thing on our minds. The temperature dropped below
freezing. The women huddled together shivering. Peter and
I shared a blanket. Filled with a sense of foreboding, we
waited for dawn.

❧

DIANA: We knew they used to put their enemies in these
containers; they'd lock them up, especially in summer,
and asphyxiate them. Sometimes they'd shoot through
the walls. Remembering this, I looked up and saw bullet
holes.

'O God, if I have to die, please just let it be quick,' I cried
out silently. 'I don't want to have to suffer pain.'

We all went in except Heather, who sat by that door all
night. Three times they tried to close it and she wouldn't let
them. The rest of us ladies huddled together, our feet like
iceblocks, trying to keep warm, trying to make it to morning.

❧

SILKE: People often behave irrationally in stressful situations. At first I was incredibly indignant, furious in fact,
that we women were lumped together with the men in one

container. It showed huge disrespect, totally contrary to Afghan culture.

Then suddenly I became afraid that the guards would barricade the door. During the months in prison I had developed terrible claustrophobia. But then I saw Georg and Heather guarding the entrance—Heather in particular knew how to assert herself. So I turned round and thought very pragmatically: *Okay, we have three blankets for eight people. The night is going to be freezing. Let's just try and organise things so that somehow we get through it.*

Dayna, Kati and I divided up the mattresses and I lay down right in the corner. At least that way I could face the wall. Kati lay next to me, then Dayna and Diana, followed by Margrit. Georg and Peter lay in the front part of the container, and Heather sat guarding the entrance.

∽

PETER: I remember at one point looking out at all the Taliban and thinking: *I've seen this on television.* I'd seen people abducted in Afghanistan and other places, and the guys walking around outside our container with Kalashnikovs looked exactly like the guys on TV.

The situation was worse because the Taliban were themselves acting under duress. They were panicking too, not sure of what they were doing. That made us even more scared. What they were doing was not measured or logical even in their own terms. That certainly didn't engender optimism.

∽

MARGRIT: When I was told to go inside the container, I immediately began to panic. *They're going to lock us in and blow us up with hand grenades!* I thought.

In a desperate attempt to stay calm, I initially found myself withdrawing from the action, looking on at the scene of confusion. Heather was locked in discussion with some of the men while Georg argued with the others, arms waving wildly in the air. Again I felt the panic rising. The strange mixture of helplessness, indignation and fear of death was like torture.

But in spite of everything, I again heard the comforting words I had heard back in the vehicle: 'Margrit, everything is okay. You're on your way to freedom!' Once I heard that, I felt calm enough to lie down quietly next to the others.

⁖

GEORG: At 6.00 a.m. Mullah Hassan returned, having clearly found a much more comfortable bed than ours. There was no tea for us and not even a scrap of food. We were bundled into the back of the Land Cruiser and our journey south continued.

Mullah Hassan had by now taken the steering wheel personally. *We're clearly quite an important catch for him,* I thought grimly.

'Mullah Hassan, what is happening? Where are you taking us?' I asked.

'To Ghazni,' he snapped.

So he was planning to stop off in Ghazni. I knew that was his home city and his family still lived there. Ghazni lies between Kabul and Kandahar in a region where the Northern Alliance had no influence. So there was no hope that anyone could rescue us once we got there.

Bumping along rough roads, the journey wore on for another three hours. The women again began reading out Bible verses and singing. I pulled myself together to listen, and in the end I started singing too. Slowly I felt a sense of calm return and I began to relax. The whole experience reminded me very much of how singing spirituals comforted the early American slaves in their captivity.

But inevitably my thoughts returned to our predicament and the immediate future. What would they do with us in Ghazni? What if they ended up taking us to Kandahar after all? I tried to prepare myself mentally for this possibility and to forge some sort of plan.

❧

MARGRIT: I was extremely relieved when our abductors returned the next morning and we continued on our journey. It was so cold in the container and I hadn't really been able to relax there at all. I was absolutely frozen.

Immediately we were back on the road, without tea or breakfast. At least our driver switched the heating on straight away. What a terrible night. It made me shudder just to think about it. I did not feel at all well. I was suffering from amoebic dysentery and felt extremely weak. There had been no toilet at the container; it had all been so degrading.

We were driving through very barren and dreary countryside. To begin with, I just let my thoughts run freely and listened to the others singing. And then suddenly that incredible sense of peace returned. I felt safe, even though, logically speaking, there was absolutely no reason to do so.

Again and again, Georg asked our driver where we were going. Finally he got an answer: we were on our way to Ghazni. We were told we'd be taken to a warm house where we'd be able to thaw out, freshen up and have some breakfast.

❧

GEORG: On the one hand, the Mullah's words were a comfort. On the other hand, we knew we couldn't trust him. We drove into Ghazni and headed straight for an ugly building with high walls and barred windows. *O God, please don't let us go to another prison!*

We all went rigid with horror as the building drew closer. Fortunately the Mullah drove past it, leaving us sighing with relief. But no, he had simply made a mistake. He turned the Land Cruiser around and headed straight for the dark entrance.

'Mullah, you promised to take us to a proper house,' I protested.

'Get out! Move!' he barked.

Immediately we were encircled by guards with Kalashnikovs. Resistance of any sort was hopeless. We had no choice but to go inside that terrible building.

Suddenly we heard explosions nearby. We knew it couldn't be Northern Alliance fighters—they were miles away. What was going on out there?

Our captors put us in two first-floor rooms that were linked together. I could hardly believe my eyes when I saw the toilet down the passage: a stinking, blocked-up hole in the floor surrounded by piles of human excrement. It was the worst I had ever seen. This was where we were supposed to live?

Then came the sound of bombing again—this time so intense that the whole building shook. In panic, one of the women in our team ran out into the corridor where she crouched down in front of the door crying.

'Get back inside!' a guard shouted at her. 'You can't stay out here!'

In complete distress, she pleaded with him to let her stay where she was. He remained impervious. I tried to reason with him: 'Let her sit there. Can't you see she's afraid? We're hardly going to escape.'

Fortunately I was able to bring him round. But by that time, all of us felt our nerves were at breaking point. We had only just escaped the air raids in Kabul and now we were suddenly in the middle of another battle—in Ghazni, of all places.

PETER: We had been tricked again. They had said they were taking us to a comfortable house where we would have access to a satellite phone. They wanted us to negotiate with our governments for money. But instead we went into what almost looked like a disused prison.

The strange thing was that we were allowed to be together, men and women. This is never the case in

Afghanistan. What was going on? They left us guarded and locked up, but many of them rushed off in a big hurry.

◈

DIANA: As we arrived in Ghazni bombs were raining on the city. The Americans knew how far the Taliban had got in their headlong flight south—all those vehicles on the road were easy to track. So America was bombing.

Mullah Hassan was in a state of panic. He just dumped us in a cell and left. We thought he had gone to get the satellite phone, but he didn't come back.

I looked at the appalling toilet, listened to the bombs falling and felt the building shaking, and I thought: *Just when we think things can't get any worse, they always get worse.*

◈

GEORG: Slowly we began to make the best of our new surroundings. The women started clearing up and laying out mattresses on the floor. We sat down and decided to start by having some breakfast. Surprisingly, the guards brought us some *naan* bread and green tea. One member of our group pulled out some leftover cheese. At least we had so far all survived in one piece.

After breakfast, we began to thank God for his protection in keeping us safe until now. Then we prayed for each other, especially for Margrit, who was very weak. The others prayed for me that I would be able to make the right decisions.

While we were still sitting together, the shooting in the city started up again. It was extremely loud and intense. Then the noise switched to the prison.

Someone ran to the window and called out, 'They're fighting right in front of the prison . . . Are they Taliban or not? . . . Lots of people are running away!'

Then everything went quiet. Not a single shot, not a sound could be heard.

The silence seemed to last an eternity. Then without warning there were dozens of people in front of the prison, trying to break down the door. Someone else ran to the window. 'There's a whole crowd of people, even some youngsters with them. They're coming in!'

In a second they'll be here! They'll storm the prison and lynch us foreigners, I thought wildly. I was petrified. My greatest fear had always been of getting abducted or lynched. I'd already witnessed a number of lynchings in Pakistan. I'd rather just be shot and get it over and done with.

Down on the ground floor, the doors were ripped open. The crowd began hammering on the door to our floor. Finally it gave way with a loud crash. Several men stormed over to our cell and yanked the door open. We were standing face to face with an Afghan fighter, sweat rolling down his face, cartridge belt slung across his shoulder and Kalashnikov waving wildly.

Totally nonplussed at finding a bunch of foreigners, he hesitated, unsure of what to do next. We stared back, paralysed and speechless.

Recovering himself suddenly, he shouted: '*Assad! Assad, ast!* Freedom! You're free!'

We could hardly believe it. 'What? We're free? Aren't you Taliban?'

'No, we've just driven out the Taliban. They're gone

now. Come out! Come out! I mean it, you're free!'

More and more men pressed their way into our cell. And slowly it dawned on us what had happened.

'Are you Massoud's men?' I asked.

'Yes, yes, we're Massoud's men!'

We turned and hugged each other for joy and relief. Some broke down in tears.

'Come out. Quickly, quickly, go now! You're free!'

We didn't need telling again. Immediately we rushed outside. The air was electric. There was still shooting going on. A rocket launcher was being set up in front of the prison.

'In here, quickly!'

With skirmishes continuing, we had to take cover inside the guard post built into the prison wall. But a short while later, we were at last free to go.

We ran as best we could, without any protection, across an open field. Finally we caught sight of the first houses where we could take cover.

One of the fighters led us through the streets. When word got around to local residents that we were there, they all came out of their homes. They peered at us in disbelief. We wandered all over the place until one of their leaders turned up and led us to his office.

The further we went, the more inquisitive the crowd became. People chatted noisily as they accompanied us: 'Who are these foreigners? Where have they come from?' No one knew anything about us.

And then suddenly the spell broke. One man threw his arms round us. Scores of people came and shook our hands and clapped us on the back. Everyone started cheering. Men came and carried our things for us.

The feeling was indescribable.

❧

DIANA: As we raced through the city I thought, *I'm not going to make it*. I hadn't had any exercise for over three months and I'd lost a lot of weight. But somehow I kept going.

We walked for about two kilometres. Everywhere people were celebrating. Women were coming to their gates without their *burkas*, waving to us in excitement. We found out later that in Kabul that morning men had lined up at the barber to have their beards cut. We noticed that many of the shops were closed; there had already been some looting.

❧

SILKE: For me, that march through the streets of Ghazni was one of the best experiences of our entire imprisonment. In a previous letter to friends back home I had written: 'One day I hope to dance with the Afghans in the streets of Kabul and celebrate with them the end of the Taliban regime.' As that hadn't worked out in Kabul, our experience in Ghazni was a real consolation.

I didn't give any thought to the fact that we weren't yet out of danger. Any member of the Taliban could have just taken off his turban, mingled with the crowd and then shot us. I was totally exhausted and yet overjoyed at the same time.

And boy, was I grateful when a man took my unwieldy bundle of blankets from me! It was like one big street party.

❧

KATI: First of all I didn't realise where we were going. I just followed the man leading us.

Then suddenly people began to emerge from nearby houses. They crowded round us. I looked into their faces and noticed immediately that they were different: they radiated hope and joy.

I had so often talked to Afghans who told me, 'There is no future for us anymore. We have no hope.' Now, for the first time since I had been in Afghanistan, I saw real hope in the faces of the people. I felt overcome with emotion.

❧

MARGRIT: For me the hours leading up to our release were like an emotional roller coaster. My feelings went up, down, all over the place. One minute we were in fear for our lives, the next we were on a high, giddy with relief and excitement.

Interestingly, a few days before, I had imagined that something like this would happen. I actually had a mental picture of a roller coaster. *Watch out!* I'd told myself. *You'll need to keep firm control of your feelings*. It turned out to be good advice.

Looking back, I'm glad it was Afghans who came and freed us. For me there was an element of healing in that. Afghans had put us in prison, but other Afghans had freed us and celebrated with us in the streets!

❧

In the sudden ecstasy of release, none of the aid workers realised that they still faced a long road to freedom. Another nightmare—as bad as anything they had been through before—was about to begin.

9

The Eleventh Hour

The aid workers were led through the streets of Ghazni by a group of proud fighters and an ever-growing crowd of fascinated onlookers. Eventually they arrived at some kind of office where they were welcomed by a man who spoke a little English.

'I am Mohammed Akhtar,' he told them. 'I'm a security official in this city.' He appeared to be the leader of the group that had driven out the Taliban.

Immediately tea was served. The foreigners were able to use the bathroom, freshen up and finally relax a little. Mohammed Akhtar was very friendly and seemed to have the situation under control. The office was packed with people. More heavily armed men were arriving all the time. Some were simply curious to see the foreigners. Others were there to take orders and immediately disappeared again.

The whole atmosphere was electric. The residents of Ghazni had clearly not been expecting this sudden liberation from the Taliban and were now unable to agree on who should assume control.

During the course of the morning, a group of wild-looking fighters stormed into the office demanding to speak to the aid workers. Mohammed Akhtar flatly refused. The two sides proceeded to yell at each other in Dari. With everyone talking at once, the foreigners barely understood a word. But the group failed to get their way; finally they appeared to give up and left.

Since arriving at the office, Georg had been observing the situation very closely and realised that various ethnic groups were vying for control of the city. Quite unwittingly, he and his team had come into the care of Mohammed Akhtar and his group. But he appeared to be well-disposed to them and made a generally competent impression. Georg was happy enough.

At about twelve o'clock they were served *kabuli palau* and all ate enthusiastically. The food tasted delicious. Afterwards they sat back and chatted, enjoying the relief of being free at last. Everyone was in high spirits.

❧

GEORG: I imagined from then on everything would be simple. I assumed we would find an office somewhere with a telephone where I could simply call the German embassy in Pakistan and say, 'Hello, we're free! Please send a helicopter over to Ghazni to pick us up.'

So I began to press our new host. 'Where can I find a telephone here?' I asked. 'It's essential that I ring the embassy in Islamabad and tell them we're free.'

'Soon, soon,' Mohammed Akhtar assured me. 'We have two or three offices in the city that have satellite phones.'

Finally we left to phone—Mohammed Akhtar, myself

and an army of bodyguards. The other seven team members stayed back at the office.

The streets were awash with people. Joy over the sudden liberation was very evident. But a definite tension was also in the air. Ghazni was home to three ethnic groups: Pashtuns, Tajiks and Hazaras. Each was now in the process of delineating its power. A lot of armed men were hanging about the place.

Many of the shops we passed had been plundered. Roadblocks had already been set up and individual shots could still be heard now and then. The mood was gradually turning. Suspicion between the various ethnic groups was returning, probably for fear of revenge attacks. This was not unjustified since the Pashtuns, many of whom belonged to the Taliban, had treated the Tajiks and Hazaras very brutally in the past.

We arrived at the official telephone centre only to find that it had already been destroyed. We continued our search, but the two other offices that apparently possessed satellite phones were all closed up. We were forced to drive back to the office empty-handed.

Mohammed Akhtar was now visibly nervous. At every roadblock, guards eyed us suspiciously before allowing us to pass.

❧

After a brief conference, Mohammed Akhtar decided to take the aid workers to one of his relatives, a man named Hamisha Gul. Gul owned a large house on the edge of the city. To get there, they first had to drive through a mainly Hazara district. Throughout the journey, they passed groups of men armed to the teeth with rifles and mortars. The driver steered the van as quickly as possible through the streets. All breathed a sigh of relief when they finally pulled up outside their new abode.

Hamisha Gul must have been a fairly wealthy man because his compound included a number of buildings. These were surrounded by high walls, as is common in Afghanistan. The foreigners were given a warm reception.

The women were shown to a room where they could rest and unwind. The room was spacious, laid out with clean mattresses and carpets. At last they could take a proper shower and relax.

∾

MARGRIT: It was wonderful to lie down and rest. We had clean mattresses, peaceful surroundings—it was a real healing experience for me. I really enjoyed the hospitality of the people. A doctor brought me tablets because I was still very weak from amoebic dysentery. The whole day passed off peacefully. We were very grateful for the care and hospitality of our hosts.

∾

DIANA: We were given a huge room as our bedroom. Being in a warm bed that night was nice.

We couldn't get used to guys coming into our room. Men from the family wanted to sit and talk to us. We had become so institutionalised that we struggled to know how to respond to them. We couldn't very well tell them to get out—after all, it was their house.

❧

While the women relaxed, Georg and Peter sat in an adjacent room, drinking tea with the Afghan men.

Eventually Georg was able to pull out his radio, which he had kept hidden in his pocket the whole time. He immediately switched on the news and learned that Kabul had fallen to the Northern Alliance the previous night, not long after they had been abducted. People had reportedly danced and celebrated in the streets. He was deeply saddened to have missed it.

He started to think again about how he might get to a telephone to call the German embassy in Islamabad. The situation in Ghazni was worrying. Time was clearly not on their side. Something had to happen soon.

❧

GEORG: I was unable to rest or relax, so I went outside into the courtyard. One of Hamisha Gul's sons, a boy of about twelve, came over to me.

'I know you,' he said. 'I saw you at the prison in Kabul.'

'What do you mean?' I asked, amazed.

'I was at the reform school for boys next to your prison and saw you when you were let out into the yard in the afternoons.'

Now I was totally perplexed. What was the son of this wealthy man doing in such a terrible place? The children and young men at the school not only received strict religious training but also were brutally beaten and tortured if they failed to toe the line exactly. We had often heard their screams from our cell.

'Why were you at the prison?'

'I did too many silly things which annoyed my father. So he sent me there.'

'What? Your father actually sent you to the prison?' What kind of fanatical Muslim must our new host be if he put his own son into such a cruel institution?

A short while later, I learned that our host had been a Talib but after the uprising had quickly swapped sides and was now working with the new power groupings in the city. He was in fact a good friend of the director of the reform school prison back in Kabul.

Suddenly I felt very uneasy. My initial euphoria turned to fear. Freedom was almost within our grasp, and yet seemingly there were more intrigues afoot.

Where had we landed? Who was trying to get control of us now?

While the other Shelter Now staff continued to rest back at the house, Georg drove into the city escorted by a group of guards. This time he was heading for the ICRC office, in the hope of calling Islamabad from there.

Georg was already familiar with the place. Three

years previously he had stopped off in Ghazni on the way to visit a Shelter Now project in Kandahar and had stayed in an ICRC guest room there. He had built up good relations with some of the staff, who remembered him immediately. The Afghan ICRC workers had been following the events of the aid workers' imprisonment and felt extremely relieved to know they were free and unharmed.

They offered Georg all the help they could give. They began by contacting the ICRC in Islamabad and asking how they could get the eight foreigners safely out of the country.

Pleased with this partial success, Georg returned to the house to wait for a reply.

That night he hardly slept a wink. He and Peter had to share a room with ten to fifteen other men who were continually listening to the radio, talking and smoking.

The Afghans took turns to guard the house. Forming patrol teams of five, they paced up and down outside. Given that it was owned by a former Talib, there was good reason to fear a Hazara attack on the building.

∾

First thing in the morning, Georg made his way back to the ICRC office. It was Wednesday 4 November.

The staff had received a reply from Islamabad. The ICRC was unable to send a helicopter to fly them out of Ghazni; it was, after all, still behind enemy lines. But the organisation was prepared to drive the aid workers back to Kabul. With the capital no longer in Taliban hands, it would be much easier to fly the eight of them out from there.

This appeared a feasible suggestion until they learned that the road to Kabul was still littered with Taliban roadblocks. If they took that route, they would almost certainly be discovered and re-arrested. It was clearly out of the question.

The ICRC staff concluded that the only other option was to contact the US forces. 'But that would be a military operation which would involve risks,' they added.

Georg considered this to be the least of his worries and agreed without hesitation.

GEORG: Finally things were moving. The US embassy in Islamabad was contacted. Staff there responded quickly and plans for our rescue began to materialise.

Owing to the unstable situation in Ghazni, the undertaking was very risky for the Americans. But they nevertheless agreed to send in helicopters with US Special Services personnel to get us out. All we had to do was arrange a place where we could be picked up.

The little office was packed with Afghans who proceeded to argue at great length as to which pick-up point outside the city would be best. Finally they reached an agreement. The Americans were informed of the location. In turn they impressed on me the need to be waiting with my team at the agreed place bang on one o'clock that night.

It was the best news I'd heard in a long time. I took a deep breath. Everything appeared to be going smoothly.

⤸

During the negotiations, a messenger arrived from Hamisha Gul's house to say that Georg and his staff would have to move to another location immediately. 'It's too dangerous out there on the outskirts of the city,' the note said. 'If a mob of Hazaras storm the house, we won't be able to give you sufficient protection. We have another house nearer the city, but your team members refuse to move without your consent. Please write them a note to say you agree to the arrangement.'

Georg could well understand the concerns of his staff. All too often they had been moved with promises of something better, only to find themselves worse off as a result. But he also understood the reasoning of his hosts and knew the situation was deteriorating all the time. He quickly wrote a note: 'It's okay for you to move to the new house. I'm still here making arrangements for us but will come to the new house as soon as possible. Things are proceeding well.'

After the remaining details had been clarified, Georg was driven back by Mohammed Akhtar and his bodyguards. The new house was a little smaller than the previous one but also surrounded by high walls. Georg informed the others of his success.

'Just imagine, by 1.00 a.m. we'll be on our way out of here!' he exclaimed exultantly. 'We've arranged a location outside the city. We're not allowed to take any bags with us, just what we're wearing.'

It was exciting news. The team were overjoyed and began discussing what it would be like to be rescued by US forces.

After lunch, Georg and Mohammed Akhtar immediately returned to the ICRC office.

KATI: We looked at our few belongings and discussed what we might be able to take with us. There wasn't much. But the few things we did have were precious to us: journals, letters, our self-composed songs, our Bibles, cosmetics.

We put on all the clothes we had. Then we began stuffing things in between the layers wherever they would fit. We had a whale of a time! By the time we were through, we looked and felt like Michelin men.

After a while, all the gear started to get in the way. Knowing we still had several hours to go, we shed a few layers.

PETER: While the women were organising themselves, I spent my time relaxing with the Afghan men. We even watched some television. I didn't have any extra gear to get together anyway. All I had was the clothes I was wearing plus a blanket.

At one point Dayna and Heather got a note from Georg asking them to come to the ICRC office. I went with them. We found Georg on a satellite phone, talking to the

American embassy in Islamabad. They wanted to hear Dayna and Heather's voices for themselves.

⤫

Peter, Dayna and Heather returned to the house and waited. By evening Georg had still not returned. Everyone began to feel a little concerned. They were all hoping nothing would go wrong at the last minute.

⤫

GEORG: Back at the ICRC office, Hamisha Gul and his Afghan entourage were waiting for us.

I had thought everything was settled, but suddenly one problem after another cropped up. Some wanted to discuss our rescue plan with the new leaders in Ghazni and clear it with them first. But others were against the idea.

'No, it's too risky,' they argued. 'The new leaders may include a few secret followers of the Taliban who will want to hand our foreign friends over. They might even start demanding money from us, assuming we've been paid for our assistance.'

It was thus essential that the operation remain a secret. No one could know that these men had helped us to freedom.

Then one of the most important men suddenly refused to take us to the agreed pick-up point. 'It's too far out of the city,' he said. 'Besides, the curfew is still in place. It's much too dangerous to travel through the city at that time of night.'

No one else was prepared to take us either. The operation was just too perilous for them. I realised that they were also afraid of getting into difficulties with the new leaders in the city.

Annoyed and disheartened, I again called the US officials. 'Guys, it's not going to work out. The Afghans here aren't prepared to go along with it. It's just too dangerous for them. You'll have to come for us by day.'

'There's no way we can do that!' came the firm reply. There could be no discussion. 'You have to leave tonight at the agreed time!'

The US forces were well aware of the extremely volatile situation in Ghazni. There was no way of predicting what would happen from one minute to the next. Arriving for the rescue operation, they could easily have got caught up in fighting between rival groups.

Because Ghazni had been liberated by an unexpected local uprising, the Americans could not count on the support of Northern Alliance troops, who were still further up-country. Ghazni was an island surrounded by Taliban territory. The Americans also knew the Taliban were planning a counterattack to retake the city. The situation was a powder keg, and time was of the essence.

Georg informed the waiting Afghans of the result of his conversation with the US officials. 'Impossible!' they insisted. Heated discussion ensued.

For the rest of the afternoon, the negotiations went round and round in circles. Georg summoned all his powers of persuasion, but he was hitting a brick wall.

He became angry and tried to appeal to their pride. 'Afghans are known to be fearless,' he said. 'How come you're so hesitant all of a sudden? Are you afraid?'

That got nowhere, so he tried a different tack. Knowing that hospitality is an extremely important obligation in Afghan society, he said, 'We're your guests: you're obliged to protect us. Please don't let us down, help us get out of here!'

Again, nothing he could say would change their minds. Finally he gave up, exhausted.

Nonetheless, the Afghans did feel obliged to do something. They began looking for new solutions. Finally they agreed on a proposal.

'Okay, we could take you to the pick-up point immediately the curfew ends at 5.00 a.m.,' they offered.

Georg again called US officials in Islamabad and put forward this latest proposition.

'Nothing doing,' they responded. 'We just can't do it. The pick-up has to be tonight at 1.00 a.m. It's your only chance. You have to persuade them. It's then or not at all!'

What could Georg say? He knew he couldn't force his hosts to change their minds. Now totally discouraged, he finished by telling the Americans that he and his team had moved to a new house, gave its location and hung up.

A short while later, the phone rang again: 'Right near the new place where you're staying there's an area of open wasteland. You could get there on foot by yourselves. We expect you there at one o'clock. Whatever happens, you have to make it there with your team!'

Georg received directions on the route from the new house to the rescue point, along with a few other instructions which were to be followed exactly.

By now it was around 8.00 p.m. In five hours, US soldiers would be coming for them. Georg had no idea how he and his team-mates were going to get past their guards in the middle of the night. Wisely, he decided to bide his time before mentioning the latest decision to the Afghans.

∽

As the local curfew had now begun, the Afghans were keen to get to their night quarters. The streets were empty except for the guards at the roadblocks. Georg's Afghan bodyguards drove with their Kalashnikovs at the ready.

After a while, a pickup full of armed men approached. The men on both sides aimed their guns at each other. Georg's blood ran cold. The two vehicles neared and the fighters eyed each other aggressively. But they passed by without incident.

Finally Georg arrived safely at the house, where the rest of his team were anxiously awaiting his return.

Tired and dejected, he sat down to tell the story.

'The Americans are adamant they can only collect us at the previously agreed time at a place near here.

But our Afghan hosts and their commander have flatly refused to let us out of the house in the middle of the night. I don't know how we're supposed to get out of here with five guards and those high walls. You have to pray! I'm going to keep trying to persuade the men here in the house to cooperate.'

In utter desperation, he appealed to the guards. 'Please, let us out! Open the gate! Our freedom is so close! Have you no mercy?'

'No,' they replied. 'We're not letting you out.' Only the local commander could authorise that, they said, and he had left.

'Then send him a message or have him brought back.'

'That's impossible. The curfew is on. We can't leave the house.'

The conversation went back and forth, but the men would not be moved. Georg refused to give up, and the men became annoyed. So he changed his tack.

'The Americans know we're here. They'll come and get us out whether you want it or not. They're on their way here now in helicopters.'

A moment later, as if on cue, the sound of a fighter jet circling the city could be heard. Now the Afghans were really afraid.

'You can't do this!' they cried. 'You're endangering our lives and those of our families. The Americans must not come.'

The owner of the house and the other men began to panic and begged Georg to do something. But they still would not open the gate. Their fear of incurring the wrath of the local commander was apparently greater than that of facing US soldiers.

Georg went over to the women and Peter. 'It's becoming madder by the second,' he groaned. 'They're just not going to let us go.'

A chorus of pleas went up as they all prayed fervently: 'God, please help us! We're so close to being free. Work a miracle and make them let us go!'

❧

PETER: I felt like praying, 'God, can't you bump these guys' heads together and get some sense into them?' It was incredibly frustrating.

The Afghans wouldn't help us, but we couldn't really take matters into our own hands because we didn't really know where we were. Even if we had somehow got out of the house, the chances of finding our way unguided to where we could be picked up seemed pretty slim.

Georg, who now had a satellite phone with him, spoke to the Americans again to explain that we couldn't get any agreement from the Afghans. But the Americans said, 'We're already committed. We're already in the air. Do whatever you have to do to get there. It's your only chance.'

❧

It was now after 11.00 p.m.—and the clock was ticking. The sense of helplessness was overwhelming and the tension became unbearable. The Afghans inside the house were panicking and pressuring Georg to do something. And all the while, any hope of rescue seemed to be melting in front of their eyes. Georg felt his head would burst.

US aircraft could now be heard clearly over the city. It was torturous.

A car pulled up outside. Someone was hammering wildly on the gate. Everyone jumped in shock. Who would come at this hour, defying the curfew? Would they be helpers or enemies?

Some of the guards went nervously downstairs. A moment later, Georg heard voices at the gate. Then he saw the local commander coming up the steps.

Thank you, Lord! he breathed.

Sitting at home, the local commander had heard the US aircraft circling over the city. It did not take much for him to work out that the Americans were coming for the aid workers after all. He intended to move the eight of them to another place as quickly as possible.

'You have to leave here immediately,' he told them. 'The intelligence officials that brought you to Ghazni have come back. They know you're here and want to kill you. Grab your things. I'll take you to a safe place.'

GEORG: I was stunned, paralysed. *Surely that can't be true,* I thought. *They're after us again? Just when we're about to be rescued? Is there no end to the terror?*

It only took a moment, but then I knew with certainty that the commander was lying. It was a trick. He knew how scared we were of our abductors, and for whatever reason he wanted to prevent our rescue.

Outwardly composed, I walked over and stood right in front of him.

'We're not coming,' I announced. 'We've had enough of this. Why won't you let us go? We're not moving. You'll just have to shoot us right here!'

In Kabul, I would never have risked such an invitation. The men there would not have thought twice about shooting us. But now I was prepared to take a risk. Somehow the people here weren't quite so callous.

Unnerved by my reaction, the commander turned away and began pacing up and down nervously. All the men started talking at once, debating wildly about what to do. All the while I stood there, praying silently and waiting.

Then the commander pulled me aside. He tried to persuade me to give in and go with him.

I calmly repeated my answer: 'You can shoot us but we're not moving.'

My iron response seemed to confuse him. He turned to me abruptly. 'Then go!' he yelled. 'Go!'

'Go where?' I asked, shocked.

'To the helicopters! Go on, go!'

What? He's letting us go? I could hardly believe it.

I shouted to the others in the next room, 'Come on! He's letting us go! Quick! Now!'

We made a dash for the gate, a string of Afghan guards in tow.

❦

MARGRIT: We'd spent the whole afternoon on tenterhooks. Our mood had continually swung back and forth between excitement about the rescue and fear that something would go wrong. By the time Georg returned it was pretty late. We could see he was exhausted.

'It looks like tonight won't work out,' he told us wearily, and briefly filled us in on the details. He left us to continue working on the guards. We returned to praying with renewed urgency.

The Afghan women who were sitting with us were afraid of what might happen to them when the Americans arrived to rescue us. When the hammering at the gate started up, they began to panic. They pulled us into the room, crying and shaking with fear. We too were close to despair.

Then I heard Georg negotiating with someone out in the yard. Suddenly he cried out, 'It's back on! Come on, we're leaving! Quickly! Just leave everything and run!'

We dashed out of the house, leaving half our things behind. Outside it was pitch black and the ground was extremely uneven. I fell down a pothole. Kati grabbed my hand and we ran on together.

❧

PETER: The journey to the pick-up point was eerie. The night was very dark because it was past curfew, so there wasn't much light anywhere. Fortunately it wasn't far. It took us about twenty minutes.

❧

As it turned out, the aid workers arrived at the pick-up point some time before the deadline. In the darkness, they formed a row as the US official had commanded and sat down to wait. The ground was frozen. The Afghan guards who had followed them waited nearby.

They waited for almost an hour in the cold. Georg stayed in touch with the Americans on the satellite phone until eventually the battery died. Fifteen minutes passed. Then suddenly they heard the roar of helicopters in the distance.

In their hurry, the group had only brought one small lamp as a signal for the Americans. But the light was too pathetic to be visible from the air, and it was also not what had been agreed with the US military officials. To make matters worse, local fighters on the lookout for the return of the Taliban were standing guard outside houses all over the city and had lit fires to keep warm. How would the US forces ever spot their light among all the others?

A short while later a huge helicopter roared overhead, coming right down low and flying just past the group.

'It was so close they must have seen us,' someone said as the machine swooped past.

'Over here!' they yelled, waving their arms wildly. But their voices were drowned out by the noise.

✑

PETER: I'd done a lot of praying beforehand, but I don't think I'd prayed as hard as then. The helicopters were only just over the houses on the side of the strip of land, less than 100 metres away. So near and yet so far.

❧

The helicopters once again gained altitude and flew off towards another part of the city. The aid workers were horrified. Had the soldiers given up? Were they leaving?

Then the big machines returned, this time flying by on the other side of them. The noise was deafening, and local residents soon started to panic. Some came over to where the eight foreigners were sitting cowering on the ground. Their Afghan guards did their best to calm the people and send them away.

❧

MARGRIT: At one point a helicopter roared just past our heads, throwing up clouds of dust. I've never experienced anything like it: the noise, the dirt in our faces. We were almost blown over by the force of the wind. The helicopters flew over us at least five times.

There was nothing we could do other than pray: 'God, make them turn round and come back. Let them finally see us!' It was enough to make you go mad.

❧

Again and again the helicopters swooped overhead in the darkness. The US forces clearly hadn't spotted them.

The situation was becoming increasingly dangerous. The curfew was a strict matter. The aid workers were sitting there for anyone to see on the edge of a piece of wasteland bordering several ruined houses. Alarm throughout the city was growing. Dogs were barking wildly. No one could fail to have heard the helicopters. They were flying so low they could easily have been shot down and the aid workers taken captive.

'It's no use. The helicopters won't find you,' the Afghan guards urged. 'Give up and come back with us. People are starting to wonder what's going on.'

'Georg, please don't give up yet,' pleaded Margrit and Dayna, who happened to be sitting next to him. 'Give the soldiers another chance.'

∽

GEORG: The sheer tension was more than I could stand. I was ready to give in to the pleas of our Afghan guards and turn back to the house.

But what would we do then? By the next day, the whole of Ghazni would know that the helicopters had been and the foreigners were still in the city. There would be nowhere else we could run to. The land route to Kabul was blocked, and it was only a question of time before our abductors would return to the city. Then we would be whisked off to Kandahar—and that would be the end for all of us.

We had to get in those helicopters, come what may. It was our only chance of survival.

I was on the verge of despair. I cried out, 'God, please help us! Please help us! Why are you allowing this?'

Our rescue was so close. We could see it—and yet it was beyond our grasp.

The emotions we all went through out there are hard to describe. I felt like a man drowning in the sea who sees a ship passing by and shouts and waves for all he's worth, but the people just don't notice him and sail on by. Eventually his strength is gone and he sinks into the abyss.

∽

SILKE: It was freezing cold. We seemed to sit there for an eternity. In my mind I was crying out to God, *God, this is it! Do something! We need a miracle! Get us out of here!*

I realised that Georg was close to breaking down. I prayed passionately for him. He needed our support. The Afghans were talking to him non-stop, trying to get him to give up and return to the house. But there was no way I was ready to turn back. All I wanted was to stay put until we were finally rescued.

∽

'We have to make a fire so they'll see us,' yelled Heather, taking off her shawl as she spoke. She dipped it in kerosene from the lamp and lit a match. She started waving it wildly back and forth in the air. The others followed her lead, setting fire to further items of clothing. The watching Afghans realised what they were doing and broke off pieces of wood from the surrounding ruins. They proceeded to build a large fire.

Again the helicopters roared toward them, straight

up the strip of land. This time the machines came so close that sparks from the aid workers' fire were blown into their faces. Heather's dress caught fire. The whole group waved and screamed. But the helicopter again retreated into the distance.

The aid workers were paralysed. At that point, most of them gave up all hope of being rescued that night. What they did not know was that one of the pilots had seen the fire this time and recognised the group.

Twenty minutes passed before the next thing happened. To the eight on the ground it seemed an eternity. Then, quite suddenly, a group of black-clothed figures emerged from the darkness across the wasteland. It took them a few moments to grasp that they were US soldiers.

'Do you speak English?' a voice asked.

After a quick head-count to check they were all present, the soldiers gave instructions. Then they were off, guiding the aid workers at a steady pace. They passed the houses and rounded a corner. Then they were tumbling into one of the helicopters. Everything around them was pitch black and the noise was deafening. But finally, they were taking off.

GEORG: The whole thing was taking much too long for my liking. As soon as I saw the helicopter, I ran on ahead of the soldiers. I fell into a ditch, scrambled out, ran on again and finally leapt into the black hole of the helicopter. I went smack into a metal wall and fell flat on the floor. Heather, who was hot on my heels, fell on top of me. I crawled on all fours. I felt numb. We had made it.

When the helicopter took off, I felt as if I was in a dream. I had no longer believed we'd ever get out of there.

The feeling was indescribable. 'I don't believe it! I don't believe it!' I kept yelling over and over again.

The rotor blades were so loud that we could hardly hear each other shout. Overjoyed, Heather crawled over to me and screamed in my ear, 'We're free! We made it! We're flying!'

~~

At 5.00 a.m. the helicopters landed safely at an airfield in Pakistan, just beyond the Afghan border. The eight aid workers were transferred to a waiting freight plane, which took off immediately. By 8.00 a.m. they were in Islamabad.

There they were met by Dayna's and Heather's ecstatic parents and by representatives from the three embassies. The eight of them were divided up and taken to their respective embassies where they were at last able to shower, sleep, eat and go shopping.

And then the press conferences began. The whole world was keen to hear of the experiences of the Shelter Now aid workers during their 105 days of captivity.

The Miracle at Ghazni

The actual rescue operation that night in Ghazni was far more dramatic than portrayed here. To avoid jeopardising further military rescue operations and to protect the identity of those in Afghanistan who assisted, the eight, names have been changed, some scenes modified and some details left out.

The Shelter Now aid workers were deeply grateful to the soldiers of the US Special Operations Force. Under the most difficult circumstances imaginable, they risked their lives to rescue them and would not give up. Equally, the team would never forget the commitment of their Afghan friends, many of whom also risked their lives to help them.

Most of all, they felt profound gratitude to God. When they finally managed to put all the pieces together, they realised that their rescue had not only been extremely risky; it had also been accompanied by some extraordinary events and circumstances. Some people may consider these lucky coincidences, but the Shelter Now workers are firmly convinced they were due to God's intervention.

- The day before they arrived in Ghazni, there were around 200 al-Qaeda fighters staying overnight in the city on their way to Kandahar. Had their abductors arrived a day earlier, or the al-Qaeda fighters left a day later, the aid workers would without doubt have been whisked off to Kandahar with them.
- The abductors from Kabul had only been in Ghazni with their hostages one hour when the local uprising against

the Taliban began. If the revolt had started any earlier, the abductors would certainly not have driven into the city, and would probably have proceeded directly to Kandahar instead.

- The uprising in Ghazni was so unexpected for the abductors and so severe that they did not even have time to collect their hostages before fleeing the city.
- A short while after the aid workers were rescued, the Taliban launched a successful counterattack and retook the city.

If the rescue operation had not succeeded that night, the eight aid workers would have immediately fallen back into Taliban hands. They felt that God, in his love and sovereignty, had brought a brief period of calm to this hotly contested city during which they could make their final dramatic escape.

Epilogue

Back to Afghanistan

Two things surprised everyone when the freed aid workers faced the press in Islamabad soon after their rescue. The first was their good physical and mental condition. The second was their statement: 'We're going back to Afghanistan. We want to carry on our work.'

Following their return to Germany after their debriefing, several of the aid workers expressed their desires more fully.

GEORG: My wife and I would like to go back to Afghanistan. We have spent the last eighteen years living in Pakistan and Afghanistan and helping Afghan refugees there. Our two sons were born and raised in Pakistan. For them it is home, and they too want to return.

During those eighteen years, I have developed a genuine love for the Afghan people. This affection grew deeper during my time of imprisonment. Tens if not hundreds of thousands of Afghans have suffered similar things. Many never made it out of the prisons alive. We believe that few other peoples on earth have suffered as much as the Afghan people.

Now that a glimmer of hope has finally emerged, we want more than ever to help rebuild this devastated land. With God's help and the support of friends, we have been able to work through the difficult experiences of those three-and-a-half months in prison and have been able to forgive those who robbed us and caused us so much distress.

∽

MARGRIT: I want to go back, in spite of all the difficulties and dangers. The experience in prison has helped me to better understand Afghans and to identify with their needs. We suffered a little of what they suffer, and I hope that will help to bring us closer together.

We now have good reason to hope that we'll be able to achieve more than previously, particularly through projects to help women. I refuse to let myself be put off and intend to meet the needs I encounter as best I can.

∽

KATI: Afghanistan is quite simply where I belong. It's often said that people grow closer when they go through hard times together. I love Afghanistan and its people now more than ever. I'm looking forward to expanding the children's project, and in particular to finally being able to take girls as well.

Afghanistan is embarking on a new beginning and I want to be a part of it. That is the work God has given me to do and what gives my life meaning.

SILKE: My work as a teacher for the other aid workers' children was only interrupted by my imprisonment. I feel I have an obligation to continue. When the families fly back to Afghanistan, I'll be on the plane with them.

I too am keen to work with the street children and would like to see more schools being built. A few weeks ago, I saw a picture of a crowd of people in Kabul printed in the *Frankfurter Allgemeine* newspaper. I happened to notice three of our street children among them. They were still wearing the shoes and coats we gave them last winter. Seeing them reminded me again how much I belong in Afghanistan.

PETER: I love the Afghan people. And I like Kabul. To begin with, I was really bitter and angry with the Taliban for treating us so unjustly. But now I find I'm able to say, like Jesus, 'They did not know what they were doing', and to forgive them as Jesus forgave his executioners.

The need is so huge. And God has not said to me, 'Stay home!' So I too am returning. What better place to employ my skills as an engineer than Afghanistan?

Since those interviews, three of the former detainees have returned to live in Kabul: Georg and his family, Silke and Margrit. Kati has married, and she and her husband Thomas have visited Afghanistan and may return at some stage. Peter has also married, but when he and his wife Rhonda attempted to return, they were unable to obtain visas.

Heather and Dayna settled back into life in the United States and continue to promote the cause of the Afghan people through their organisation, Hope Afghanistan.

As for Diana, long before her imprisonment she had reached the decision to spend some time at home in Australia before moving to work in another country. But when she stepped off the plane in her home city of Perth, she was so inundated with requests to speak about her experiences that her plans changed. She now shares her story and the lessons it taught her around Australia.

Just two months after the aid workers' rescue, Georg, now back in Germany, received a telephone call from a friend in Afghanistan.

'Mr George, I slaughtered a cow and three sheep yesterday,' he began. 'I invited all the tribal leaders in the area for a big celebration. All of them praised Shelter Now's work and said they want you and your people to come back to our province as soon as possible.'

He told Georg that the leaders had decided to send him a letter formally inviting him to restart Shelter Now's aid projects in their province. 'I'm going to send you the invitation immediately,' he concluded.

Sure enough, a short while later the invitation arrived. Georg knew most of the leaders personally. In the Khost province, Shelter Now had produced over 100,000 concrete roof beams and sold them at rock-bottom prices to local people. One of the signatures came from a man who attended the 2001 UN conference in Bonn on rebuilding Afghanistan's political system.

Wednesday January 9, 2002

To Shelter ~~Known~~ International

Germany

Many many greetings from Khost tribal leaders to head of Shelter now international (Mr. George) From along ago there was your project of Guarders, which was lead by shelter now International And these project was very Helpful to Khost people, As you have information that Afghans people Have seen many problems and suffered in many fighting, but It was very helpful Project for Khost Tribal people. But we re get to say that this project was looted and was closed by Taliban and It was dark age . but nowadays situation is very excellent than anyother time and today we have a big Meeting in Khost about your project. And we have decided today to Invite formally shelter now International to take part in the rehabilitation of Khost province, we suggest for you to open a project in Khost as soon as possible and also we love germen people very much. Because they have Served to khost people very well, before also there were a lot of projects and now also; but we know Mr. George Head of shelter now and he is a kind, noble and helpful person and we know him very well and he can work better than anyother person and project, because he is familiar with our culture we would like German people very much and they know our problems very well and they can work better that anyother people. And we hope that you will never forget Afghans people . Especially Khost people.

It is true that you have seen many difficulties and you were in Jail. And we were very very unhappy , but we couldn't help you on that time. Because the first people were khost people. Against of Taliban and now we will sign these letters. We love Mr.Goerge very much .

Love to Mr.Goerge a head of shelter now International and German People.

1. Sayder Jan	2. Haji Shaswer Khan (Tanai)
3. Naeem (Kochai)	4. Haji Wazir (Mangal)
5. Abdul Qayoom Khan	6. Mirbadod (Tanai)
7. Shah Khan (GurBuz)	8. Dr.Mohammad Din Gul
9. Haji Sher Gul (GurBuz) (Khostwal).	10. Deputy Governor of Khost Province Mustafa
11. Governor of Khost Badshah –Khan (Jadran)	
12. Speaker of khost showra and province (Khostwall)	

Despite on-going dangers, Shelter Now has returned to Afghanistan to continue its work.

Shelter Now's Work Before 2001

Before the arrest of the eight aid workers and their sixteen Afghan colleagues, Shelter Now had large projects in the Pakistani refugee camps. It built simple mud houses, provided food, and supplied refugees with drinking water and firewood in winter. When the war in Afghanistan started following 11 September, all the expatriates working in Pakistan had to leave the country. Shelter Now's Afghan employees carried on the project activities in the camps.

In Afghanistan, Shelter Now worked in Kabul and in seven different provinces. It had factories producing concrete roofing materials in the cities of Jalalabad, Khost, Kandahar and Helmand. Thousands of concrete roof beams and slabs made in these factories helped the people reconstruct their houses.

In Herat, Shelter Now had started to work in one of the largest refugee camps in the world, housing around 300,000 refugees fleeing drought. The organisation had large projects in the province of Ghazni where it employed up to 1800 Afghans to repair the centuries-old underground water systems called *kareezes* (see diagram p 248). It refurbished a few thousand wells, dug many new ones, and cleaned and repaired the underground channels that connect the wells together.

In Logar the organisation had just finished a clinic, and prior to that it had built 500 houses (these were destroyed during an earthquake some years earlier). In Kabul, where its main office was located, the project for street children supplied them with food and clothes and taught them various skills.

When the Taliban began to arrest Shelter Now personnel, those who were not detained fled to Pakistan to avoid arrest. The Taliban looted almost all of Shelter Now's factories and offices and even the houses of all the expatriates. This was a difficult loss for both the organisation and individuals.

In March and April 2002, most of the Shelter Now expatriates who had been in Pakistan returned to Peshawar to continue their work. Among them were Greg and Shelvi Gilmore, leaders of Shelter Now in Pakistan, who had cared for the Shelter Now members who managed to flee Afghanistan the previous August; and Len Stitt, the former deputy director of Shelter Now in Afghanistan, with his wife Diane.

At that time, Shelter Now ran a staff retreat in Pakistan to which most of the people who had previously worked in the region came. Georg, Marianne and their two children were there, along with Silke and others. They had returned to Pakistan with the goal of re-entering Afghanistan and rebuilding their work. Even while they were in jail, most of the Shelter Now workers had prayed that they would be able to take up their work in the country again.

Len and Diane were the first to return to Kabul, in April 2002. Then on 23 June the Taubmann family, together with Silke and others from the former Kabul and Peshawar teams, drove back into Kabul. Margrit also joined them to continue her work as Georg's secretary.

This they did even in the face of threats from the Chief Justice of the new government, who had declared he would put the former prisoners on trial again if they re-entered the country.

❧

GEORG: On our return to Kabul, our first task was to find new houses. Most of our homes had been looted and other people were living in them. We opened our office again, and in a short time our work was firmly established.

We began to work in a few villages north of Kabul in the Shamali Plain. These had been completely devastated by the Taliban—thousands of houses had been lost. The villagers had taken refuge in Pakistan, where Shelter Now had built a house for every family and supplied them with food. When they heard that Shelter Now was returning, the elders approached us and we promised to rebuild their villages.

We constructed more than 300 houses and dug fifteen wells. A school and community centre were built and *kareezes* repaired. At the same time, we erected a large factory in the area that was producing thousands of roofing beams and slabs after only a short time.

A village of one hundred houses was rebuilt in the

province of Logar. In three sectors of Kabul, wells were dug and others repaired. In an area where all the *kareezes* had been completely destroyed, water started to flow again after we cleaned several kilometres of channels and repaired hundreds of wells.

In another area of Kabul that was frequently flooded by rain water and melting snow, we built a sewerage system to prevent a residential area from being deluged. We also made large distributions of food to very poor and needy people. During our first month, Shelter Now received more than US$1.5 million from donors for our relief and development projects.

All this work was achieved in less than a year following our return to Afghanistan.

On 5 August 2002, one year to the day after his arrest, Georg was spending some time reflecting and praying about the event that had changed all their lives. Suddenly Marianne burst into the room.

'Georg! Daniel's school has been attacked by terrorists!'

Shortly after returning to Kabul, Georg and Marianne had sent their eldest son, Daniel, to boarding school in Pakistan. They were visiting the area themselves when the school was struck by Islamic extremists wanting to kill as many children as possible.

Georg rushed to the scene. There was blood in many places. Six men, five Pakistani employees of the school and one local villager, had been killed, but all the staff and children were alive. (A book called *Angels in the Rafters* was later written about their miraculous escape.)

This event shocked all those with students at the school to the core. They never expected anybody to target their children. Many expatriate aid workers, including Shelter Now members, struggled with the question of whether it was right to carry on under such dangerous conditions. The school itself was relocated to another country.

Starting up again in Afghanistan, the team has faced overwhelming challenges. Yet among the sad events, many encouraging things have happened. They have been especially heartened by the welcome they have received from many Afghans, including tribal leaders and influential members in the country's new government. Georg has even been visited by some of his former Taliban jailers. At one time they guarded him with Kalashnikovs, but now they come to ask him for jobs. A number of other former Taliban still come to see him.

Next he plans to work in a province which has been devastated by the drought. The villages he will be working in will include the village where the director of one of the prisons in which he was fiercely interrogated lives. People who live in these areas have come to request help to rebuild their villages.

❧

GEORG: It was very painful in the beginning to return, something that cost me more strength then anything before. We had a lot of resistance. We stood before our looted house as a family and everything was gone. Yet God has been faithful to us.

Our return has left a deep impact on many Afghan people. Wherever we have been, people have recognised us and greeted us with great joy. The government has also welcomed us back. Many of the Afghans who suffered terribly under the Taliban regime have a great sympathy for us because we have suffered as they have.

But they are surprised that we have returned. We are thankful to God for giving us the strength to forgive those who harmed us, to start again, and to continue to serve the Afghan people with the same love and dedication we had before.

The Shelter Now team has plans to set up projects even in areas that are known as former Taliban strongholds. Already they have begun work in Kandahar and are planning to move back to Khost and Helmand, still areas with a lot of Taliban influence and violence.

The team's hope is that this will demonstrate their love and commitment to these people no matter what their past has been. And their prayer is that they can work for many more years to build up this country and to demonstrate the love of God to the Afghan people.

The traditional *kareez* irrigation system

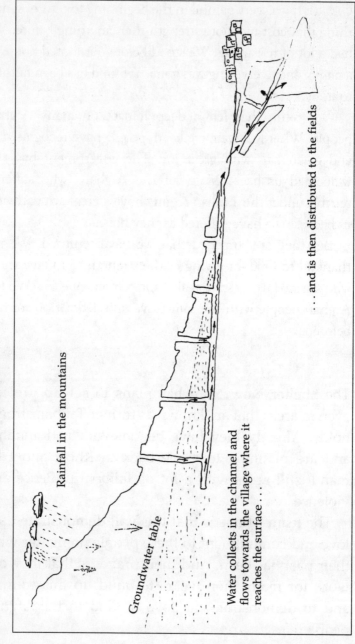

Rainfall in the mountains

Groundwater table

Water collects in the channel and flows towards the village where it reaches the surface . . .

. . . and is then distributed to the fields

105 Days in Captivity— A Chronology of Events

Day 1: Friday, 3 August 2001

Two Shelter Now aid workers—Heather Mercer and Dayna Curry—are invited to an Afghan family. They take small gifts and show a documentary film about the life of Jesus on a laptop computer. Dayna has to leave early to go to another appointment. Her taxi is intercepted by the Vice and Virtue Police. She is arrested. Two hours later, Heather leaves the house and is also arrested as she climbs into a waiting taxi.

Day 2: Saturday, 4 August 2001

The remaining Shelter Now aid workers in Kabul meet to discuss the situation and pray. They take precautionary measures in case further employees are taken in for questioning or their premises searched.

The German head of the team, Georg Taubmann, visits a high-ranking member of the Taliban whom he has befriended, in the hope the man will be able to use his influence to help solve the problem. But the women were arrested by the Ministry for the Prevention of Vice and the Promotion of Virtue, which operates independently. The Taliban official can do nothing.

Day 3: Sunday, 5 August 2001

The Shelter Now offices in Kabul are searched and property is confiscated. Georg along with two of his secretaries, Margrit Stebner from Germany and Diana Thomas from Australia, are arrested. Peter Bunch, an Australian engineer, is also arrested.

The head of the children's project, Kati Jelinek from Germany, and her housemate, Silke Duerrkopf (Daniel and Benjamin Taubmann's home tutor), are arrested at home.

A further sixteen Afghan employees are arrested and sixty-four boys from the children's project are locked up in a reform institution.

Day 4: Monday, 6 August 2001

Georg's wife Marianne is able to escape by land to Pakistan with their two sons and all the remaining non-Afghan Shelter Now staff. Most of the organisation's aid projects are destroyed.

Day 9: Saturday, 11 August 2001

The Taliban release all sixty-four Afghan boys originally arrested with the aid workers.

Day 11: Monday, 13 August 2001

Diplomats from Germany, Australia and the United States fly to Kabul but fail to gain permission to visit the detainees.

Day 12: Tuesday, 14 August 2001
Representatives of the Taliban publish 'evidence' in support of the charges against the aid workers. The material even includes crucifixes, such as are common in Catholicism but not at all in keeping with evangelical Christianity. Taliban officials speak of several thousand video cassettes on Christian teaching and 10,000 Bibles, which they claim to have found in the Shelter Now office. These were, however, never produced for public scrutiny.

Day 19: Tuesday, 21 August 2001
Following fruitless efforts to gain access to the aid workers, the Western diplomats are forced to leave Kabul. The Taliban refuse to extend their visas.

Day 24: Sunday, 26 August 2001
A delegation from the International Committee of the Red Cross, including two doctors and a nurse, receives permission to visit the aid workers in prison.

Day 25: Monday, 27 August 2001
The German, United States and Australian diplomats, along with the father of Heather Mercer and mother of Dayna Curry, are allowed to visit the detainees for the first time.

Day 33: Tuesday, 4 September 2001
The aid workers' trial begins in Kabul without their knowledge. No public access is granted.

Day 37: Saturday, 8 September 2001

The defendants are brought without warning or preparation before Afghanistan's Supreme Court. They deny any wrongdoing.

Day 38: Sunday, 9 September 2001

Afghanistan's Foreign Minister Wakil Ahmad Mutta-wakil announces the Taliban might consider swapping the eight aid workers for an Islamic militant jailed in the United States.

The Tajik guerrilla leader Ahmed Shah Massoud is killed in an attack carried out by suspected al-Qaeda operatives. The death of the highly respected leader is a heavy blow to the Afghan Northern Alliance in its ongoing fight against the Taliban.

Day 40: Tuesday, 11 September 2001

The terrorist attacks on New York and Washington. The situation of the eight detainees changes dramatically. All hopes of a quick release are abandoned. As each day passes, the chances of them ever getting out of the country alive diminish.

Day 42: Thursday, 13 September 2001

Diplomats, UN officials and relief agency staff leave Kabul along with the relatives of the two US citizens inside the prison. The eight detainees appear to be the only Westerners left in Afghanistan.

Day 46: Sunday, 17 September 2001
Lawyer Atif Ali Khan, from the Pakistani border city of Peshawar, is commissioned to represent the aid workers in court. He is an expert in *sharia* law.

The eight detainees are moved suddenly and without explanation to an intelligence service prison.

Day 59: Sunday, 30 September 2001
The aid workers make their second appearance before the Supreme Court. This time they are accompanied by their lawyer, Atif Ali Khan. The charges are read out in Dari only. As a result, neither the defence lawyer nor the defendants are able to understand.

Day 63: Thursday, 4 October 2001
The charges are made public. The lawyer immediately goes to work on his defence.

Day 65: Saturday, 6 October 2001
The Taliban offer to release the eight detainees if the United States abandons its threat of military action and enters negotiations. US President George W. Bush rejects the offer.

Day 66: Sunday, 7 October 2001
US and British forces begin bombing Afghanistan. The detainees are in grave danger of being hit by stray bombs or of being abducted or lynched by al-Qaeda mercenaries.

Day 72: Saturday, 13 October 2001
The aid workers' Muslim lawyer submits his written defence to the Supreme Court.

Day 80: Sunday, 21 October 2001
The detainees are moved to another prison—the infamous 'Riasat 3'—just for the night. This becomes a regular practice. The measure is allegedly for security reasons.

Day 81: Monday, 22 October 2001
The Pakistani lawyer Atif Ali Khan receives no response to his defence and is turned away at the court. 'The Supreme Court has more important things to attend to right now than worry about the detainees,' says Chief Justice Noor Mohammed Saqib.

Day 84: Thursday, 25 October 2001
The lawyer and the foreign embassies in Islamabad lose all contact with the aid workers. The eight are completely cut off. Their relatives and Shelter Now staff outside Afghanistan have no idea how they are doing and fear the worst.

Day 102: Monday, 12 November 2001
The trial is adjourned until further notice. Kabul has suffered heavy bombing. Northern Alliance troops are about to march in and take the city. The hostages are abducted from the prison. Their captors want to hide them in the Taliban stronghold of Kandahar.

Day 103: Tuesday, 13 November 2001

During a stopover in the city of Ghazni, the hostages are incarcerated in the local prison. But a sudden uprising organised by local residents forces the Taliban to flee, leaving them no time to collect the hostages.

The aid workers are freed by local opposition fighters. With the aid of the ICRC, they make contact with their embassies in Islamabad by satellite telephone.

Day 105: Thursday, 15 November 2001

In a dramatic night-time rescue operation, the aid workers are airlifted out of Afghanistan by US Special Forces and flown to Islamabad.